contents

W9-BIY-821

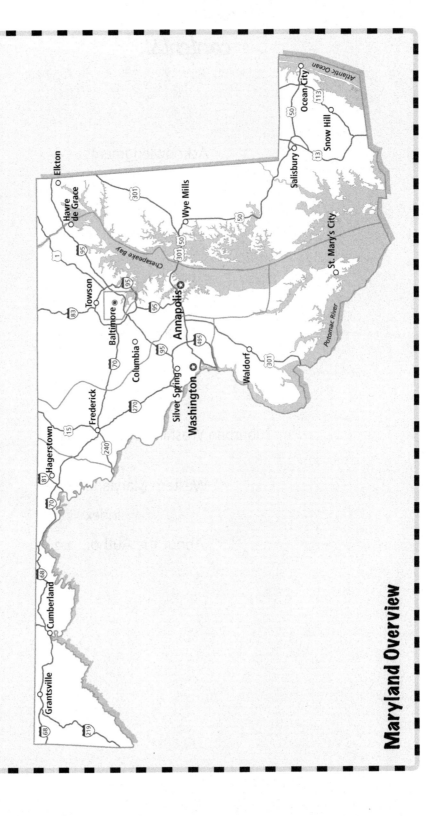

Maryland Overview

Curiosities Series

Maryland CURIOSITIES

Quirky characters,
roadside oddities &
other offbeat stuff

Allison Blake

Guilford, Connecticut

The prices, rates, and hours listed in this guidebook were confirmed at press time. We recommend, however, that you call establishments to obtain current information before traveling.

To buy books in quantity for corporate use
or incentives, call **(800) 962-0973**
or e-mail **premiums@GlobePequot.com.**

Copyright © 2009 by Morris Book Publishing, LLC

ALL RIGHTS RESERVED. No part of this book may be reproduced or transmitted in any form by any means, electronic or mechanical, including photocopying and recording, or by any information storage and retrieval system, except as may be expressly permitted in writing from the publisher. Requests for permission should be addressed to The Globe Pequot Press, Attn: Rights and Permissions Department, P.O. Box 480, Guilford, CT 06437.

Photos by Allison Blake unless otherwise noted

The poem "Ode to the Equinox" is used by permission of Jefferson Holland, Poet Laureate of Eastport.

Project manager: John Burbidge
Text design: Bret Kerr
Layout: Casey Shain
Maps: Daniel Lloyd © Morris Book Publishing, LLC

Library of Congress Cataloging-in-Publication data is available on file.

ISBN 978-0-7627-4130-4

Printed in the United States of America

10 9 8 7 6 5 4 3

acknowledgments

*A*mazing, how well my brain's now trained to smoke out the curious. And I owe it all to many, many good people who helped by offering great ideas. Patiently, I might add. Thinking up curiosities takes time.

Many more folks than I can list contributed to this book with information, directions, and otherwise good-natured assistance.

A huge thanks to writer Beth Rubin and photographer Sara Morell, "tour guide" Karen Myer, Vanessa Parks, Baltimore in-the-know types John Ziemann of Baltimore's Marching Ravens band and Fell's Point aficionado Mark Walker, Baltimore folklorist Elaine Eff for inviting me to the screening of *The Screen Painters,* Joe and Joey Kro-Art/Kroart of Ocean City's Ocean Gallery, Connie Yingling at the Maryland Tourism Department, Sara Hisamoto of the Baltimore Area Convention and Visitors Association, Susan Steckman at the Annapolis and Anne Arundel County Conference and Visitor Bureau, and public relations experts at tourism bureaus across the state.

Thanks also to Joe Evans at *PropTalk* and Jeff Holland at the Annapolis Maritime Museum, Susan Meredith of Blackwater Paddle and Pedal Adventures, and Rhonda Aaron. Ann Garside at the Maryland Historical Association, various folks at the University of Maryland, and Kevin Dodge at Garrett College were all a big help. So were numerous curators (what a great job!) and public relations folks who work at museums, gardens, historic houses, parks, quirky sites, and, as we say in the curiosities biz, other offbeat stuff.

My own family was full of good sources, especially my mother, Miriam Blake, and my mother-in-law, Anne Stinson. The former has been in D.C.'s Maryland 'burbs for years, the latter in Baltimore and on the Eastern Shore. They were ready with the memories and deep perspective when a sounding board was required. Thank you.

As always, Joshua, thanks for being patient. Hi Sinta!

The mother ship for artistic curiosities:
the American Visionary Arts Museum in
Baltimore. SARA MORRELL

introduction

S ay what you will about Maryland, it's certainly not beige. No, in fact, it's color coordinated. Three of our official state animals confirm this fact. Go look at a Baltimore oriole, a calico cat, and a checkerspot butterfly—they're orange, black, and white. Officially, the animals were chosen because they match the colors of the Maryland flag.

Have you seen our flag? It's quite flashy—if red and gold instead of orange, but what the heck. It coordinates. Our founder, the Lord Baltimore, left the design to us by way of his coat of arms. Two quarters are black and gold for the Calvert side of his family. The Crosslands—his mother's people—gave us the red and white. The designs are very different, and yet together, they work. And that may say as much about our diverse state as anything. We've got very different regions, but together, they work.

Some have even called us "America in Miniature" because we have everything within our borders. We have oceanfront, lowlands, piedmont, mountains, rivers, suburbs, big cities (well, one), medium-size cities, small cities, towns, crossroads, and, maybe best of all, we have the Chesapeake Bay. Sure, we have to share it with Virginia—the mouth of the bay lies within its borders—but most of the nation's largest estuary is right here in the Old Line State. I read on the Maryland state tourism department Web site that we don't have desert, but I know a professor in Western Maryland who knows where to find cactus clear out there.

Curious to find out more?

Here in Maryland, we have Annie Oakley's retirement home and Babe Ruth's birthplace. And where else does a neighborhood "secede" from the state capital and get away with it? Are you aware that a museum devoted to our nation's most secret agency (that we know of) is right in our midst? Or that the likely inspiration for *Uncle Tom's Cabin* lies within our state's borders?

Let's look at our firsts. The first bomb-dropping device was tested from an airplane in Maryland. The first commercial ice-cream production started in Baltimore, and the first disposable bottle cap was made in Baltimore. The country's first umbrella manufacturer set up shop in the city, and the nation's first gas streetlamps lit up there, too. Marylanders built the first monument to George Washington that was started and the first one that was finished. In 1813 the world's largest single-span bridge straddled the Casselman River, a marvel at the time. We also put the nation's first bookmobile on the road.

We have the birthplace of American railroading.

You've probably heard about the blue crabs we eat. But some of us also eat ham stuffed with kale. This is a very uncommon dish, exclusive to Southern Maryland.

We've got a town called Accident. And, of course, we've got Baltimore, where folks flock to a two-night extravaganza called Night of 100 ELVISes, make sure they don't miss the wild holiday lights consuming two sides of one neighborhood block, and got so mad when the Baltimore Colts left town in the dark of night that the Colts' marching band played on for another eleven years. In early May, folks in the city dress up and go watch giant sculptures that can handle water or land race for 13 miles—and you should see the enormous pink poodle! That city's got spunk. They also have a very nice museum devoted to public works that shares a building with a working pumping station. Really.

If you're looking for a garden to relax in, we've got one in Monkton with lots of giant topiary. When was the last time you closed your eyes and smelled fresh-cut yew in the shape of a peacock, or Winston Churchill's hat? Speaking of Churchill, I heard a little tidbit about him: He played the jukebox at the Cozy Inn in Thurmont. Who can beat that?

We're America in Miniature, and we've got good curiosities. Now go check 'em out—and have fun while you're at it!

1

The Eastern Shore

You might say Maryland's Eastern Shore is a bit out there. Literally. It dangles off to the east, separated from the rest of the state by Chesapeake Bay. The Maryland shore takes up the lion's share of the Delmarva Peninsula, although Delaware and Virginia also get their bits of turf.

Unless you were up for a very long hike, you could only get there (or around there) by boat for the first 300 years after Europeans arrived. So, it's fair to say the locals developed a strong independent streak. You can still find ample evidence of that. Take the four-time women's world muskrat-skinning champion. She worked hard for the title.

Trappers and watermen (the Chesapeake name for fishermen) show off their professional prowess in goose-calling championships, or by pitting their favorite hard-shell crabs against one another at an annual race. In Ocean City, the Victorian-era boardwalk defines the beach town. A few imaginative folks and venerable family businesses—like Trimper's Rides, in biz since 1887—resist the tide of condominiums and refuse to be swept off the boardwalk with the morning sand.

The Eastern Shore was "discovered" when the Chesapeake Bay Bridge opened in 1952. City slickers from Washington, D.C., and Baltimore no longer had to take a ferry or drive around the northern end of the Chesapeake. Leaving their suits and subdivisions behind, they began to arrive in droves and discovered what the farmers, trappers, watermen, and local landed gentry always knew—it's nice over there.

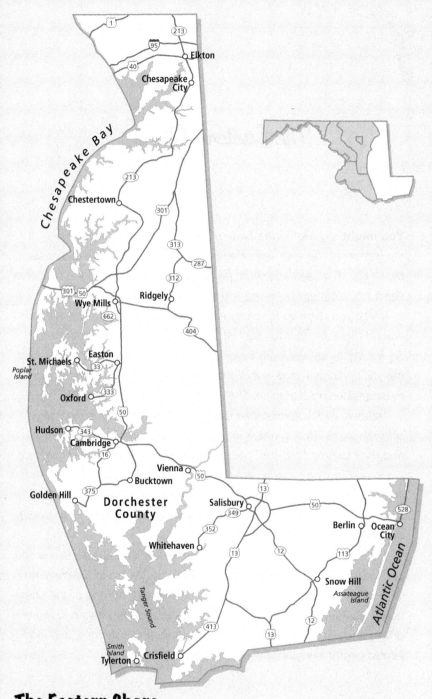

The Eastern Shore

Reining in the Crowd
Assateague Island

Wild ponies still roam free on Assateague Island, which straddles the Maryland-Virginia line. For upwards of 400 years they've roamed, descended from shipwreck refugees or forebears left by settlers to graze. They've bred with abandon and trampled their habitat because, after all, they're thoroughly at home. Scientists, of course, don't always like that. They're looking at the big picture. Herd sizes need to be managed or ponies die of starvation and islands get damaged.

So back in 1988, scientists executed what appears to be the first-ever successful birth control program for wild horses that used a particular type of vaccine. This took place on the Maryland side of the island. As an expert explained to me, the vaccine is now available for other fertile herds of, say, white-tailed deer, or wild mustangs out west. Even elephants. Dart guns inject the vaccine into the mares. Over time, the Assateague herd is expected to drop from 134 down to somewhere between 80 to 100 ponies. One unintended consequence: Mares that aren't foaling annually are living longer and healthier lives.

If you go to Assateague, you may well spot a pony on the beach, or even in the campground. If so, guard your gear. After learning to stomp through Styrofoam coolers, they've now figured out how to open the hard-sided kind. You're well advised to leave the ponies alone. They're cute and look harmless but, after all, they're wild.

The office for Assateague Island National Seashore is located at 7206 National Seashore Lane in Berlin, but it might be easier to find out more about this large, two-state park by checking it out at www.nps.gov or calling (410) 641-1441.

Taming the "Wild" Child
Berlin

Little boys in black cowboy hats gallop past, members of the *Shrek* generation. They don't know Hoss Cartwright from the Lone Ranger, but who cares? Frontier Town, located at 8428 Stephen Decatur

3

★ ★

At Frontier Town near Berlin and Ocean City, the West has been winning for decades.

Highway, has been a popular destination since it opened in 1959. You can talk Westerns with their parents and grandparents here, strolling memory lane while Junior learns the joys of cap guns.

And learn them they do. A kid doesn't need to know *Maverick* to kick up his cowboy boots in front of the Yank 'Em and Pull 'Em Dentists in this 1860s-style Western storefront town. Nearby stand the Longhorn Saloon, the Cowboy Store, and the Twin Cheeks Bathhouse. A model of an 1880 steam train whistles as it pulls out of the Old #44 Train Depot. A stagecoach stops for passengers. There's even a rodeo.

Here comes Wyatt Earp . . . Is that Doc Holliday? Gun-slinging actors play out an Old West drama in the dusty street, and then some lucky buckaroos get to join a reenactment of the reenactment. Each child is assigned to one of the actors. They face off and stride toward one another. When cap guns are drawn, the men and boys open fire. And the lone girl, pink cowgirl hat bobbing on her head, jumps up and down.

That's Frontier Town—at least, that's the Western theme portion of this large complex that includes a water park and campground. It's open from mid-June through Labor Day. To find your way to the Western theme park, go to www.frontiertown.com or call (410) 641-0057.

A Considerable Weight

Bucktown

Born a slave in south Dorchester County, Underground Railroad conductor Harriet Tubman began her heroic career after a violent incident in a corner store that still stands.

It all began when she was only thirteen, on a day she'd spent stripping leaves off vine-like flax. It's said her hair looked like a "bushel basket," since she'd been running her hands through it to disentangle leaves. When her master asked her to go to the Bucktown Village Store to pick up dinner supplies, she responded as any woman would: She couldn't go when her hair was a mess. So she found her mistress's shawl, covered her head, and then went to the store.

As she and another customer shopped, a slave boy ran in. Close behind was his overseer, who tried to enlist Harriet's help so he could catch the boy. Harriet refused, and gave the overseer a piece of her mind. That's when the boy made a break for the door. The overseer threw a weight from the store's scales at the runaway and missed, hitting Harriet instead. As a result, she suffered from narcoleptic episodes for the rest of her life.

The store's present-day owner, Jay Meredith, descends three generations from the man who bought the store in about 1860. Jay and his wife, Susan, tell me that was about twenty-five years after this incident, recorded in the Tubman biography *Bound from the Promised Land* by Kate Clifford Larson.

Harriet felt she took her instructions for leading slaves north directly from God during her sleeping spells. She also believed that God used the shawl to save her life, because without it, the weight could have killed her. In the end, conductor Tubman escaped north but returned to the land of her birth nineteen times to lead slaves north to freedom.

The Bucktown Store is headquarters for the Merediths' Blackwater Paddle and Pedal Adventures, located at 4303 Bucktown Road. Reach them at (410) 901-9255, or visit www.blackwaterpaddleandpedal.com.

Pistol Packin' Pensioner
Cambridge

When sharpshooter Annie Oakley retired from Buffalo Bill's Wild West Show after seventeen years, she and her husband, Frank Butler, settled on the Eastern Shore, of all places. The couple's retirement didn't last long, however. They stayed in their redbrick home from 1913 to 1915 before she returned to public life. Guess Cambridge was too quiet for pistol-packing Annie. The house is privately owned so you can't peek inside, but a large sign at 28 Bellevue Avenue lets passersby know they've found the place.

Annie designed the house herself, adding touches like a roof that allowed her to shoot game on the Choptank River from the window. The house lacked closets, but that didn't bother her. She said that she'd lived out of trunks her whole life—why change now?

Known as "Mrs. Butler" in Cambridge, Annie generally kept to herself, though she gave shooting demos to the local Girl Scouts. The Butlers also liked to pull a particular prank on their guests that went like this: As Annie sat on the porch, Frank would take a visitor out for a row on the river. When Frank put a cigarette between his lips, she'd shoot it out from her porch perch. "That's just Mrs. Butler doing a little spring cleaning," deadpanned Mr. Butler.

Local resident Mary Handley, an Annie Oakley reenactor who's studied her life (and generously shared her knowledge with me), points out that the Cambridge home is the only one that Annie lived in that is still standing. When asked why she thought Annie's retirement didn't last long, Mary replied: "She wasn't the kind of person to stay settled, I don't think."

A Passage to Delaware
Chesapeake City

In 1824 construction finally started on the Chesapeake & Delaware Canal, located at the north end of the Delmarva Peninsula. This was nearly 200 years after a Bohemian mapmaker first came up with the idea. You see, it's a short trip across the narrow peninsula right there, and shaves 300 miles off the route up Chesapeake Bay between Baltimore and Philadelphia. So, for 75 cents a day, 2,600 men finally swung pick and shovel.

Ocean-going vessels take a 300-mile shortcut from Baltimore to Philadelphia via the Chesapeake and Delaware Canal. DAVID HAWLEY, US ARMY CORPS OF ENGINEERS

★ ★

Go to Chesapeake City for a good view of the 14-mile canal, and hang around long enough to watch one of the gigantic oceangoing vessels pass through. These 1,000-footers pass beneath a 140-foot-clearance bridge that arcs over the canal. An engineer told me that about three huge ships pass by each day. Lots of tugs, barges, and smaller craft use the canal, too.

The canal bisects Chesapeake City, which itself grew out of the canal's birth. Check out the southern half, just a few blocks long by a few blocks wide, with streets lined with Victorian houses painted multiple hues. At the edge of town stands a small museum located in the original canal pump house. The best way to find out how to locate it is by checking www.nap.usace.army.mil/sb/c&d.htm.

A Spot of Tea
Chestertown

When it comes to famous tea parties, Boston gets the history book glory. But Chesapeake Bay saw its tea-stained Colonial moments, too. In Annapolis, the tea-toting brigantine *Peggy Stewart* was burned by her owner the year after the Boston Tea Party, part of a deal reached when the ship arrived with its unwelcome cargo. And in Chestertown, in the spring of 1774 the locals banned the leaf in their town. To underscore their determination—or so the story goes—they went to the Chester River, raided the *Geddes,* and dumped the brigantine's tea into the drink.

Today, look for the tricorn hats at the annual Chestertown Tea Party Festival over Memorial Day weekend. Saturday's events include a game of "Toss the Tory," in which town dignitaries fill in for authentic Tories, and a re-enacted tea-dumping into the Chester River still takes place. On Sunday, wacky rafts resembling cars or creatures vie for the Tea Cup during the festival's annual regatta on the river.

It's a lovely drive to Chestertown. Take U.S. Highway 50 east over the Bay Bridge to exit 25, Route 213 north, and continue 18 miles to the town. To find out all about the festival, go to www.chestertowntea party.com.

Tallulah Bankhead rests
in peace near Chestertown.

Too Fabulous for Words

Chestertown

Daaaaahlings, have you wandered through a Colonial graveyard recently? You simply must! One never knows who's buried there. Take, for example, the venerable cemetery at St. Paul's Parish, over 300 years old. Here lies larger-than-life Tallulah Bankhead, talented star of stage and screen. She never hesitated to speak her bright and witty mind. Sometimes trolling the gutter to make her point, she scandalized folks from Europe to the United States.

The Alabama native's father was speaker of the U.S. House of Representatives, and her sister, Eugenia, lived on a farm outside of Chestertown. Upon Tallulah's death at age sixty-six in New York City, Eugenia brought her to Maryland to rest in peace. Word is that Tallulah vacationed on the Eastern Shore at her sister's place, so it makes a certain amount of sense that she's buried here. You'll find her grave in

the northeast section of the parish's "New Cemetery." The sisters lay side-by-side beneath marble slabs under a big tulip poplar near a small lake.

For more about the church and cemetery at 7579 Sandy Bottom Road, call (410) 778-1540 or visit www.stpaulkent.org/churchyard.htm.

Hot Crabs
Crisfield

Years ago, when Crisfield native Paul Emely was a teenager, he and a buddy spent a whole week training a Maryland blue crab to race.

"Some crabs are 'swimmers,'" he explained. "They attach to poles instead of crawling on the bottom. For some reason, they're quicker. We caught this one in particular. We had a little float we kept him in. We'd take him out and put him on the hot road, and when he hit that hot road he took off. We knew we had a winner." Unfortunately, this "winner," who'd trained for the National Hard Crab Derby, was disqualified due to size.

Training crabs for the race may be a dying practice, but folks still go to great lengths to put on the National Hard Crab Derby & Fair over Labor Day weekend. Heck, they've been doing it for more than sixty years, and there's a ton to do and see, including swimming races and workboat-docking contests.

A newspaper editor proposed the festival's centerpiece race in 1947. If Kentucky can host a horse race, he reasoned, why can't Crisfield, aka "Crab Capital of the World," run the crabs? The first derby took place the next year in front of the post office. Back then, the crabs raced out from the center of concentric circles. Today, a specially designed wooden track is trucked over to a bleacher-flanked area called the "Crab Bowl." With white numbers shoe-polished on their shells, the crabs break out of a starting gate and scramble for the finish. Several heats lead to the finals.

If you want to compete but don't have a crab, no worries. For a nominal fee, you can purchase a crab and enter the race. For the same fee, you can also enter the race and bring your own crab. But if you need a crab, get there early. Racing crabs usually sell out before 10:30 a.m., hours before the 2:30 p.m. starting gun. The big event takes place on the grounds of Somers Cove Marina on Seventh Street. To learn more about the weekend fest, call the Crisfield Chamber of Commerce at (800) 782-3913 or visit www.crisfieldchamber.com/crabderby.htm.

All Hail
Easton

Those guys in camouflage baseball caps up on the stage? They're "hailing." You'll also hear them issue a "come on." And when they "lay down"? Well, it's not for a nap.

They're demonstrating the language of goose at the World Championship Goose Calling Contest, one of five bird-calling contests at the Waterfowl Festival in mid-November. This festival shows all sides of Eastern Shore culture, from the hunters in the field to the bejeweled art-buyers at this world-class wildlife art festival. In 2006 somebody paid a record $124,000 for a painting.

One champ calls Easton the "Super Bowl of Goose Calling."

"The outside community looking in would view it as quirky, but there's something very addictive about communicating with a wild animal," said two-time world champion Kevin Popo, a hunting guide from nearby Delaware. "It's hard enough to get your dog to sit. Now take a wild animal and try to get him to 'sit.'"

The goose-callers converge from all over the United States to display their fluency in the language of goose. Essentially, they pretend they're in a hunting blind in the field and honk imaginary Canada geese in their direction. They "hail" a goose from a far distance. The "come on" means callers work pitches to sound like more than one goose. The "lay down" comes as the goose decides to land. These are all official judging criteria, and the winner of the senior division takes home $10,000.

That's some serious money. Maybe the champ will spend it on wildlife art.

To get to the festival, follow the geese or, from D.C. or Baltimore, drive east on US 50 across the Bay Bridge and continue into Easton. Call (410) 822-4567 or go to www.waterfowlfestival.org for more information.

The More Things Change
Easton

Some things just don't change. Back in 1682, work to create the now-historic Third Haven Friends' Meeting House was authorized. And what happened? Construction lagged behind schedule. Quaker minutes from the era indicate the universal response to slow contractors: complaints.

Once the meetinghouse opened in 1684, the equality-minded Quakers divided the space. The idea was to give women their own meeting space equal to the men's.

Then came the critical year of 1730. Once again, the more things change, the more they stay the same. The building needed repairs, especially the roof. Of course, there was a contingent who wanted to start from scratch and build a bright, shiny, new meetinghouse. Thank heavens more sensible heads prevailed. A new roof was installed, and the building at 405 South Washington Street (410-822-0293; www .thirdhaven.org) lives on.

These tales were shared with me by a gentleman who's long attended the meetinghouse. It is the country's oldest documented wood building that has been continuously used for religious purposes, and is open to the public. It is built of beautiful wide oak planks. The building also is unheated. So, in winter, the local Quakers move over to the heated "new" brick building, built in 1882.

The four-time women's world muskrat skinning champion, straight from Maryland's Eastern Shore, may be showing her skills at the annual Outdoor Show in February.

Muskrat Love

Golden Hill

When January comes, Rhonda Aaron knows where her son and husband will be—in the marsh trapping muskrats. Why? Because they love her. Aaron's the four-time women's world muskrat-skinning champion. A girl's got to practice.

Understand that this is part of the family livelihood. The meat is cooked, and pelts are sold to furriers and usually shipped to Russia. It's integral to life in southern Dorchester County, inhabited by trappers, farmers, and watermen.

"I've grown up around it my whole life. I never thought it was different," said Aaron.

Aaron first picked up a knife to skin a 'rat when she was a child for a very simple reason: When you live in the country and the hunters come home with dinner, somebody's got to cook it. Sacks filled with muskrat (or goose, or duck, or deer) come into the kitchen and are placed on newspapers on the kitchen linoleum, and dinner preparations begin.

As for becoming a competitor? That started in the 1990s, when Aaron was active with the National Outdoor Show. The show, held in February at the South Dorchester Pre-K–8 School, delivers the true-blue local goods. Not only do the muskrat skinners compete, but so do the log sawers, bird callers, and pole skinners. The community even crowns Miss Outdoors, and you can learn all about it at www.nationaloutdoor show.com.

As Aaron watched only three women compete in the muskrat skinning one year, she decided she'd take up the competitive knife. Skinning takes upper body strength; you've got to lean into it. She practiced, and moved closer to the top spot with each passing year. Judges at the competition look for speed and the quality of the pelt—no nicks accepted! In 2008 Aaron achieved her best-ever time by skinning three muskrats in one minute and twenty-four seconds.

Usually, skinning goes faster at home than on the stage. Which makes a certain amount of sense because, as we all know, there's more than one way to skin a 'rat.

Incoming at one of Ocean City's many curious miniature golf course holes.

Crash Landings
Ocean City

Don't run off Coastal Highway when you catch the yellow prop plane out of the corner of your eye. It's only pretending to crash land at Hacker's Lost Treasure (mini) Golf Course at 139th Street and Coastal Highway (410-250-5678). Ocean City's numerous minigolf courses are full of exotic holes. You'll see Spanish galleons, winged creatures, and knights atop a multipastel castle. There's a giant planet (I think). Volcanoes smoke. Falls run with red water. Indeed, creatures seem to emerge from various multicolored lagoons.

As for the yellow plane: It's a refurbished Beech 18, engineered to sit atop a fake rock cave. It's making an ersatz crash landing above dinosaur bones poking up from the lagoon below. The tale of Ole Professor Hacker, an imaginary explorer, leads you through the course. The treasure? You had fun.

Since 1902, this dragon has circled aboard Trimper's carousel on the Ocean City boardwalk.

A Family's Jewel

Ocean City

Hewletts and Packards make computers. Fords make cars. Trimpers? They make summer memories on the Ocean City boardwalk, a family specialty going back to 1887.

You'd be hard-pressed to find a Maryland family without at least one member who's taken a spin through Trimper's Rides. In 1902, when the Trimpers bought a Herschel-Spellman carousel, the company sent carvers to complete the forty-five animals, including a tuxedo-clad frog and lion among the horses. The Trimper family cherishes the "Rose Horse" because it was named for one of their own. Then there's the animal whose genus (or is it species?) seems to be open to interpretation. When curators from the Ukraine arrived decades back to refurbish the carousel, they thought the green dragon was a shrimp.

A steam engine once powered the carousel, then electricity arrived. Legend says the old engine was too heavy to remove, so it was buried. It may lie under the bumper car floor.

Inside the building on a busy summer night, pipe music blares. Barkers use the carousel as transportation, hopping on and off with ease. Managers respond to health emergencies or ride to the other side of the building in a jiffy. Grab your clan and go round together at Trimper's, South First Street and the Boardwalk (410-289-8617; www.beach-net.com/trimpers).

Why Change?
Ocean City

No wonder Donald Fisher Jr.'s grandfather decided to sell popcorn when he opened his stand on Ocean City's boardwalk in 1937. The puffy treat managed to stay popular even during the Depression, when popcorn was one of the few goodies a family could afford.

According to the Popcorn Board—yes, there is such a thing—street vendors pushed steam- or gas-powered poppers through fairs and parks as early as the 1890s. Today, Mr. Fisher's descendants carry on the tradition at the same corner, Talbot Street and the Boardwalk. Developers once tried to sell the family a bigger building that would include their store. The family just said no, reasoning, if it ain't broke, don't fix it. "They wanted to have the air space above us," said Fisher. So their seventy-something-year-old popcorn legacy (Saks Fifth Avenue once carried Fisher's Popcorn!) carries on. The new building? It has risen around them.

You can't miss Fisher's Popcorn on the Boardwalk. Their formal address is 200 South Boardwalk (410-289-5638; www.fisherspopcorn.com).

★ ★

It's Astounding!

Ocean City

Joe Kro-Art is called the "P.T. Barnum of Fine Art." If you have any doubt, visit his Ocean Gallery on the Boardwalk at Second Street. There's a black "Batmobile" parked on the street side, a creative midnight-to-6:00 a.m. art car project undertaken with his son one night. Items from sixty-eight different buildings around the country "shingle" the gallery's sign-plastered facade. The turkey roaster on the building painted to look like an eye once belonged to Joe's wife. Ocean Gallery (410-289-5300; www.oceangallery.com) acquired its signature slogan—"It's Astounding!"—after Joe overheard a patron marvel at the place.

The impresario of the astounding Ocean Gallery, a can't miss Boardwalk stop, makes art fun.

Here's the thing: For all the wild stuff, folks find and buy art here. From fabled Baltimore photographer Aubrey Bodine's work to pre-Raphaelite-looking pieces to Marilyn Monroe posters, the Boardwalk landmark is an endless warren packed with art of all types.

"Fine art should be fun," said Kro-Art (which is the family name minus the hyphen and capital *A*). That's the point: It makes folks feel that art is approachable, and they can have fun with it.

Kro-Art's local antics are legendary. Another art car, the "Titanic," retrofitted for environmental purposes, now lies on the Atlantic floor. It's part of the the Ocean City Reef Foundation's artificial reef. Joe and his henchmen filled it with dry ice, and steam poured from the windows as it sank. In one of his local TV commercials (of which there have been many), a dummy on a bicycle is pushed off the gallery roof. Cut to the boardwalk. Up jumps lanky Joe, arms outstretched.

The Ocean Gallery's been packing 'em in for decades, and Kro-Art has now been joined in business by his son. "People always ask me, 'When are you going to do the commercials?'" said Joey. When he was single, no way would he subject himself to the risk of ridicule from the ladies. But now that he's happily married? "We'll see."

Saved in the Sand

Ocean City

Summertime strollers along Ocean City's boardwalk have come to expect him. No, not Him, but a latter-day disciple who spreads His Word, very simply. Artist and minister Randy Hofman sculpts sand with biblical expression.

From the beach along the Boardwalk at Second Street arise his intricate messages. ALL ARE WELCOME read the words beneath a highly detailed Last Supper. Each sculpture takes ten to fifteen hours to make, and Hofman has come to count on volunteers from various groups to help. At night, lights shine on the sculptures. A tip jar stands alongside. If you want to see more of Hofman's sand sculptures and other art-works, check out www.randyhofman.com.

★ ★

Scriptures in the sand stand along the Ocean City boardwalk.

For more than thirty years, Hofman's been at it. Like many, he vacationed in "O.C." as a kid, so it's no surprise that the former advertising-art student ended up here. In the early 1970s, another guy was sculpting biblical sand sculptures. Hofman helped him out—a disciple, as it were. Later, he took over the enterprise. Along the way, Hofman learned that Elmer's glue gives sand sculptures (and their scriptures) life beyond daily tides.

"They're temporary," Hofman said. "Like us."

Sands of Time . . . and Place

Ocean City

Here's the thing about sand: The more you've traveled, the more you've seen. Sometimes the sand is kind of rough. Sometimes it feels like sugar. Bermuda's beaches are pink. On Hawaii's Big Island, they're greenish. Sand's basic compounds must come in different colors, or mix with other stuff to create its rainbow hues. Ponder this at the Ocean City Life-Saving Station Museum's expansive display of sand samples from around the world.

The display began when a visitor walked into the museum, located at the southern end of the Boardwalk, and announced that he thought

Sand samples from across the globe are on view at the Ocean City Life-Saving Station Museum.

Ocean City had the prettiest sand anywhere. Why didn't they prove it? So the museum began requesting sand from beach towns all over America. The idea caught on, and visitors and locals started bringing sand back from their travels. Samples are displayed in a glass case. There's volcanic Iwo Jima sand brought back by a World War II vet. Sand from White Sands National Monument in New Mexico, which is pure white. Sand from Provence, France, which looks like cinnamon. More than a hundred samples span the globe.

While you're here, take a look at bathing suits through the decades and other beach-related exhibits at this fine small museum. It's housed in the town's former Life-Saving Station (the Coast Guard's precursor), which was moved to the Boardwalk. Call (410) 289-4991 or go to www.ocmuseum.org for more information.

Going with the Flow

Oxford

Talk about a sight gag. Just for fun, eighteen Mini Coopers once crowded aboard the nine-car Oxford-Bellevue Ferry when over the rise came vacationers from North Carolina. They were looking for a ride across the Tred Avon River. And what were they driving? You guessed it: a Mini Cooper.

That amusing moment was but a blip in the centuries-long life of the ferry, thought to be the country's longest-running privately owned ferry. It goes back to 1683 and connects Oxford with Bellevue, a stop en route to popular St. Michaels. One Richard Royston earned 2,500 pounds of tobacco in the seventeenth century to operate the ferry. In the next century, a widow who outlived three husbands kept the boat going.

This area is full of can't-get-there-from-here Chesapeake creeks and rivers, so its residents have long used rivers as roads. Imagine the ferry's importance for basic transportation.

By 1886 the ferry operators replaced sail and oar power with a small coal-fired steam tug. In 1912 came a gasoline-powered tug. Diesel

Down on the Feline Farm

Islands used to stud Chesapeake Bay. One, called Poplar Island, lay off Talbot County. It was a little place with a life so healthy that the federal and state governments are currently resurrecting it. They're churning sand dredged from Baltimore's channel into what was left of the island. However, that tidbit is incidental to our tale, which dates to the 1840s and one of Maryland's most storied families.

Gripped by depression following the War of 1812, the agricultural area was prone to the occasional hare-brained money-making scheme. According to Dickson J. Preston's *Talbot County: A History,* an ad seeking female black cats was placed on behalf of Charles Carroll, grandson of the first Charles Carroll, a Marylander who signed the Declaration of Independence. Seems Carroll the younger had heard about a Chinese market for black cat fur. He thought he'd create a black cat fur farm on Poplar Island, which he owned. After all, the felines would have room to roam and plenty of fish for food. But Mother Nature had other plans. A hard freeze arrived. When ice formed on the bay, the cats, no dummies, headed for shore.

And so we are left to wonder: Are the black cats of Talbot descended from hearty survivors? I heard from one source that they might have ended up in nearby Sherwood, but that's all I know.

power arrived with another ferryboat in 1950. Nowadays, passengers are more likely to be tourists or locals short-cutting around US 50. But you still may encounter a local driving a tractor or bulldozer. The ferry plows on.

Hours are 9:00 a.m. to sunset from March through November (just Fridays, Saturdays, and Sundays in November). To check schedule details, call (410) 745-9023 or go to www.oxfordbellevueferry.com.

Fly One On
Ridgely

I was in southern Louisiana once and needed to research tractors. I asked the salesman how the thing handled on a hill. "It can climb that," he said, pointing across the concrete lot to an itty bitty incline.

Anyone who knows the Eastern Shore's terrain can appreciate why that story came to mind when I heard about a hang-gliding school at 24038 Race Track Road (410-634-2700; www.aerosports.net) in Ridgely. I thought you needed a mountain, or at least a real hill, to get one of those things aloft. I thought wrong. It turns out that a hang glider needs a hill like a skier needs woolen knickers.

Through the magic of aero towing, you can hang glide anywhere. All you need is the right powered ultralight, 250 feet of regulation tow rope, and proper training. "It flies nice and slow," said Highland Aerosports co-owner Adam Elchin. "The aircraft acts as an engine until we get to altitude."

As a result, the school has flourished for a decade in flat Ridgely, and has taught folks as young as thirteen how to solo. A student's first flight is aboard a tandem with a teacher. Elchin is so reassuring that even those afraid of heights might be tempted, because, he says, technology has created a trusty glider that won't fall out of the sky. "That just doesn't happen," he said. A bar controls your speed.

First-timers head up for fifteen to forty minutes; more ambitious flyers take lessons. If you meet with too much wind on the day you're scheduled to fly, not to fret: You can grab a Kitewing and a Dirtsurfer, equipment that lets you "windsurf" down a runway.

They stock cool toys at the hang-gliding school.

Pork in the Park

Salisbury

Sandy Fulton had never judged a barbecue contest before, but in 2004 she learned fast. During the "whole hog" portion of the program, she peered into the grill to find a cooked pig wearing a string bikini and lei. Talk about presentation!

The Pork in the Park Bar-b-Que Festival she runs as Wicomico County's tourism director has taken off like a squealing sow. From fourteen competing teams in 2004, the April event quickly grew to fifty-eight

Pullin' pork at Pork in the Park in Salisbury has become a rite of spring. WICOMICO COUNTY DEPT. OF RECREATION, PARKS, AND TOURISM

★ ★

teams and drew a crowd of 15,000 to Winterplace Park by 2007. It's also officially sanctioned by the Kansas City Barbecue Society (KCBS), which strictly controls blind barbecue judging with a system involving computers, lidded taste samples, and tight rules. For instance, there's no fraternizing with the contestants, and judges must "reject unapproved garnishes." They're not kidding around. Becoming a certified KCBS barbecue judge has become so fashionable around Salisbury that Fulton sponsors a training class. Salisbury's best-known corporate citizen, Purdue Farms, donates birds for the chicken barbecue competition

Just Desserts

Key West may have its lime pie but, boy, does Maryland have a cake. A really good one. So good that the Maryland General Assembly recently named Smith Island cake the state's official dessert.

Heaven for icing enthusiasts, the cake comes with umpteen thin layers—sometimes as many as twelve. "People always say, 'How do you get those thin layers?'" said Mary Marshall, one of Smith Island's bakers. "They're baked individually." And no, she reports, they are not cut with dental floss, as she's sometimes asked.

For generations, Smith Island cake was the province of cake walks, church suppers, and family gatherings on Maryland's only unattached, inhabited island, an insular watermen's enclave with a strong Methodist streak. In-the-know types, especially on the lower Eastern Shore, knew how to find the special cake on the mainland: at a restaurant with Smith Island connections, perhaps, or through a friend whose mother lived on the island.

Then came a time when Mother Nature stumbled. She wasn't working and gives out the Purdue in Excellence Award. (Because, after all, the Delmarva Peninsula is Chicken Country.)

Serious barbecue competitors stay up all night while the pig roasts, usually twelve to fourteen hours. "You're constantly wondering what your temperature is," said Jerry Elliott, a Salisbury barbecue icon. "Although they have equipment now so I can control that cooker anywhere, via the Internet."

Who knew? Apparently, everybody over on the Eastern Shore is finding out. If you want to learn more, check out www.porkinthepark.org.

---

her usual magic with the Chesapeake Bay crabs the islanders depend on. An economic boost was in order, and that's how the state dessert campaign began in 2008. Things shifted into high gear when a call came from the capital: "I need cake up here in two days for everyone in Annapolis."

Legislators, lobbyists, and probably the shoe-shine guy in the capitol building must have lurked in doorways to snatch another slice of Smith Island cake. There were slices on carts, slices on wagons. "We peddled cakes from the security guards to the senators," said Julie Widdowson, a Lower Shore tourism honcho who was deeply involved.

Then came the hearings, the press, the this, the that, and, of course, the other thing. When the governor finally signed the cake into legislative history, a cheer went up across Chesapeake Bay. But it was a long legislative winter, and a lot of hard work. "Over here," Marshall told me from her island home, "we say, 'It weren't no bed of roses.'"

To find out how to get hold of a cake, contact Widdowson through the Somerset County Department of Tourism at (800) 521-9189. You can also try Marshall at (410) 425-2023.

✫ ✫

It Takes a Village
Snow Hill

Way back when, iron smelters noted that newly poured iron, cooled in its molds, looked like pigs—piglets at their mama's teats, to be exact. Rectangular bars extend from a larger central bar. And that, dear readers, is how pig iron got its name.

Bog ore collected in swamps was once smelted into pig iron at the Eastern Shore's only furnace. Had you stumbled, cold, upon the towering, oversize brick structure—as folks did during its century-long abandonment—you might have wondered, "What the heck?" It looks like it should be perched on a medieval heath, shrouded in a swirling mist. The enterprise that flourished here from 1830 to about 1850 sent its finished product down a now-dry canal to Nassawango Creek and Chesapeake Bay.

It took a village to make the iron at Nassawango Iron Furnace. Today that village has been re-created as Furnace Town at 3816 Old Furnace Road (410-632-2032; www.furnacetown.com). Take a gander at the museum church, kitchen gardens, and blacksmith shop that holds demonstrations, some housed in small, historic structures that have found new life here. In the museum you'll find a seated sculpture of a freeman named Samson who arrived with the furnace owners in 1837. He lived on the property, and then stuck around after the place was abandoned in the 1870s. He died in a local almshouse, purportedly at the ripe age of 107.

A 1930 fire ravaged what remained of the decrepit village, including the owner's mansion. Old photos from the early twentieth century show smiling families on outings to the abandoned furnace. Come see for yourself daily from April 1 to October 31. The rest of the year, you can stroll the grounds during daylight hours.

Honk Three Times

You don't want to get lost in the marshes of South Dorchester County, sometimes called the "Maryland Everglades." That happened to me once, back in the pre–cell phone era. The car's gas tank lit empty, and the sun was sinking fast as dark clouds rolled across the late October sky. Talk about spooky.

Thank heavens I didn't know about Big Liz. According to legend, a slave owner with a Civil War–era treasure waded into Greenbriar Swamp with his slave, Big Liz. She buried the treasure, and he nailed a spike into a tree to mark the spot. Then he cut off Liz's head to keep her quiet. Her ghost still haunts the swamp. Reportedly, head in hand, she continues to guard the treasure.

The locals have nailed the ritual for raising Big Liz. Go out to the De Coursey Bridge over the Transquaking River at midnight, flash your car headlights three times, honk the horn, and wait. A friend took her son there one Halloween and saw a glowing orange ball hovering over the swamp. "Very weird and I did not like it," she said. (Reportedly, this could have been "marsh gas.") Another local went with his family. They got spooked and left—but saw nothing.

Another woman I know, who is nothing if not sensible, found herself driving through the swamp late one night when a low moan arose from the backseat. She thought maybe a drunkard had crawled in for a nap. She looked around and saw no one. Because there's no place to pull off, she had no choice but to drive and drive. The moan continued until finally she reached US 50 and civilization. The next day, friends at work declared Big Liz the source of the noise. Who knows? I've heard that in fairly recent times, loggers working the area, unaware of the tale of Big Liz, felled a massive tree with a spike in it.

Defense Central
St. Michaels

Imagine Mrs. Merchant's surprise when, carrying her infant down the stairs, a British cannonball bounced ahead of her. It came in through the roof, courtesy of the War of 1812. Her lovely brick home at the edge of St. Mary's Square remains a St. Michaels landmark, privately owned and therefore off-limits to visitors.

A few houses over from Mrs. Merchant's stands a cannon that townspeople used to defend themselves against the British on August 10, 1813. St. Michaels is known as "The Town that Fooled the British" because, as the redcoats arrived, residents raised the town's lanterns, fooling the British into shooting low and missing its targets. Mrs. Merchant's roof was the only casualty.

St. Michaels now is a capital of Eastern Shore tourism, full of shops, restaurants, and charm. The cannons are a reminder of the days when regular folks like shipbuilders and watermen dominated local life. To find out more about this lovely spot, check out www.stmichaelsmd.com.

Getting as Far Away as Possible
Tylerton, Smith Island

To reach Tylerton on Smith Island, Maryland's only unattached, inhabited island, you must drive about three hours from Washington, D.C., or Baltimore to Crisfield, catch a boat (daily at 12:30 p.m., year-round), and cross Tangier Sound. The boat ties up at Tylerton—itself a little island—where you'll find the Inn of Silent Music.

This lovely B&B gives new meaning to getting away, because it's got a place where you can press even farther away from civilization as we know it. Down a path from the inn is "The Greenhouse" on stilts. Check out the waterfowl from one of two decks. Or go inside the room and settle in, knowing you've gotten as far away as you possibly can.

To learn more about the inn, call (410) 425-3541 or visit www.innofsilentmusic.com. If you need ferry info, call (410) 425-2771 or check www.smithisland.us.

A getaway's getaway hides on Smith Island—itself a getaway. ROB KELLOGG

Button, Button . . .

Vienna

Elliot Island sits at the marshy edge of the middle of nowhere. About seventy folks live 26 miles away in the hamlet of Vienna, once a Colonial port on the Nanticoke River, off US 50 near the intersection of Routes 731 and 331. A few years back, the locals opened a museum in town at the former Hurst Brothers Service Station and Confectionary Shop. Featured are buttons from Elliott Island's gone, but not forgotten, Martinek Button Factory.

A mom-and-pop operation, the Martinek factory opened when its namesake family arrived from New Jersey in 1949. It closed in 1999, the last stateside button factory, squeezed shut by international competition. In between, workers transformed Australian mother-of-pearl into buttons via a seven-step process on a machine you can see at the museum. Occasionally, a docent demonstrates the machine's operation, and you can find out when by contacting the Vienna Heritage

Buttons made in the marsh at the Martinek
Button Factory are remembered at the Vienna
Heritage Museum. TOM BRADSHAW

Museum at (410) 376-3442 or visiting www.viennamd.org.

Did you know that "blanks" are stamped out of shells like cookies
out of rolled dough? From a blank, you can make up to four buttons.
A three-part chemical bath can create smoky-gray buttons. Even better:
You can make sequins.

The Martineks did just that. Look closely at costumes once worn by
Elvis Presley. Those are Martinek sequins. "You know Elvis wouldn't
put on a little plastic button," said Daniel Martinek, who obviously
takes pride in his family's legacy of producing mother-of-pearl buttons.
Barbie (yes, Barbie) wore the last of the factory's commercial sequins.

Fixin's
Vienna

Care to guess what shad planking is? Sounds like some kind of floor-
board repair. But it's not. Shad are the largest members of the herring
family, and the fact you may not have heard of them helps explain why
the planking takes place.

Here along the Nanticoke River, where American shad once teemed like cod used to off Massachusetts's famous cape, an annual "planking" held the last weekend of April raises awareness about the fish's dwindling population. Locals from the Chicone Ruritan Club get together and start hammering. No, not to repair the floorboards. They nail marinated shad steaks to oak planks, and then grill them over an open fire. The cooking starts about 4:00 a.m. By noon, lunch is ready, served with a heapin' helpin' of here's-what-you're-missing.

Proceeds from the Nanticoke River Shad Festival & Planking help fund restoration of the river's shad. The festival is co-sponsored by the Town of Vienna, the Nanticoke Watershed Alliance, and the Chesapeake Bay Foundation, and you can find out all about it at www.chicone ruritan.org.

Coming Home to Roost
Whitehaven

In the course of my research, I ran into a man who works in a chicken house by day and a chicken house by night. A former chicken house, that is, when it comes to the latter. Let me clarify: The Red Roost, at 2670 Clara Road (410-546-5443; www.theredroost.com), was converted from one Eastern Shore staple—the chicken house—to another—a crab house—back in the 1970s.

My source is a chicken farmer who plays piano at the Red Roost's Wednesday-night sing-along, a scene you've got to see. Folks waiting for their all-you-can-eat belly-busting meals belt "Danny Boy" beneath lights fashioned from crab baskets.

So, I asked the pianist: What of the old working chicken house remains in the restaurant?

"It's still got the rail for the feed line," said one-half of the Backfin Banjo Band. "The metal rail in the center of the house. You hook a feed cart to it, fill the feed cart, and go feed the chickens. It's in the ceiling. You hang the feed cart, like a gondola at a ski lift."

That device hails from the days when chicken farmers still fed chickens by hand. A fellow named Frank Valentine built what's now The Red

Roost and raised chickens. It's said that another fellow, named Frank Purdue, used to deliver feed. The late chicken magnate's truck reportedly tended to get stuck in the low-lying area. Then another fellow took over and opened a campground in 1971. The chicken house morphed into a recreation room/general store and then, later, a crab house.

"On any given night," said co-owner Tom Knorr, "you'll see anything from a tractor to a Rolls Royce in the parking lot." At the tables? Their owners, plowing through all-you-can-eat clam strips, shrimp, ribs, and fried chicken. And, of course, crabs.

Flour Power
Wye Mills

A schoolteacher with an industrial streak, Ruth Orrell started selling one of Maryland's few native foodstuffs door-to-door during the Great Depression. Her efforts led to Orrell's Maryland Beaten Biscuits, the state's last commercial source of these small, hard biscuits. They're even made in Ruth's old kitchen.

Ruth used to get up before dawn to make the dough—an unleavened variety dating to the plantation era—before heading to her one-room school. By the time she got home, hired ladies had finished the baking.

Today, Betsy Orrell Skinner looks around at the simple kitchen she's known all her life. No, she reports, not much has changed since her grandmother's day. Well, the microwave is new. An Esskay tin of lard sits atop a shelf. The heavy cutting table Ruth beat her dough on was long ago replaced by a specially designed beater that's decidedly low-tech. The ladies around the table in the back room swap stories as they roll the dough and form the biscuits.

Biscuits, biscuits, and more biscuits have been a constant in Orrell family life. Betsy's father, Ruth's son Dick, had a military career spanning the globe and came home to the family business. At one point he tried to engineer a production machine, but no luck. The ladies roll on.

The price of a dozen has risen to $4.50 from 15 cents back in

At Orrell's Maryland Beaten Biscuits, the ladies roll on.

Ruth's day. Look for them on traditional Maryland holiday tables. To order them, call (410) 822-2065 or visit www.beatenbiscuits.bizland .com/index.html.

From an Acorn

Wye Mills

Whoever heard of a state park consisting of a lone tree? Not me, until I heard about the Wye Oak, which took root in the 1500s. It stood before the European settlers arrived. The state bought it in 1939, making it into Wye Oak State Park (on Route 662, 1 mile from the intersection of Routes 50 and 404; 410-820-1668).

We Marylanders never thought the Wye Oak would leave us, though from time to time—like in the 1950s—a big storm took away large limbs. But time waits for no tree. On June 6, 2002, an enormous thunderstorm felled the Wye Oak, the country's largest and maybe even oldest living white oak. At the time, the tree was 21 feet, 8

inches wide and 96 feet tall, wearing a 119-foot crown. This led to an odd situation. The state park—all twenty-nine acres—remains. Sure, there's a little brick house and the cool nearby gristmill and it's nice to picnic by the nearby stream, but isn't the park about the tree?

A fence surrounds the Wye Oak's massive stump. In the middle grows a brave lil' thing. Poets herald mighty oaks, and old states like Maryland apparently try (at least in some regions) to never forget. Ergo, if you stop in Wye Mills to view the great Wye Oak, just go with the flow when all you see is a wee Wye oak, a descendant of the original. And give it 500 years or so. It'll grow.

From a mighty white oak—the Maryland state tree—grows this lil' guy.

2

Baltimore

Anyone who knows *Baltimore understands that writing about the city for a book of curiosities is, as they say, like shooting fish in a barrel. It's as cool as the Baltimore Colts beating the New York Giants for the 1958 NFL Championship. As hip as a hundred Elvises.*

Why is this old industrial port so quirky? Who knows? But if there's a Johns Hopkins University student looking for a thesis topic, I've got an idea. How about researching immigrant neighborhoods, customs brought from the old country, and a blue-collar ethic, and how they percolate over 275 years? Throw in an oceangoing history launched from the nation's north-south border and a string of world-class industrial firsts. Your professor's gonna give you an A.

In Baltimore, if the pigs aren't running at Pigtown, the "hons" are humming through Hampden. You could easily spend more than a day going through the city's curious museums, where you'd find George Washington's dentures, a train locomotive from every era possible, and a historical overview of how trash has been picked up in the city's streets. If you have Baltimore sports heroes on your mind, why not visit the room where Babe Ruth was born? From there, you simply follow baseballs painted in the street to get to the museum that displays the bed in which Johnny Unitas was born.

I know an alley where there's a hundred-year-old barn full of horses. Matter of fact, I know where there's a hundred-year-old guy (almost— he's ninety-nine now) who presides over a film festival.

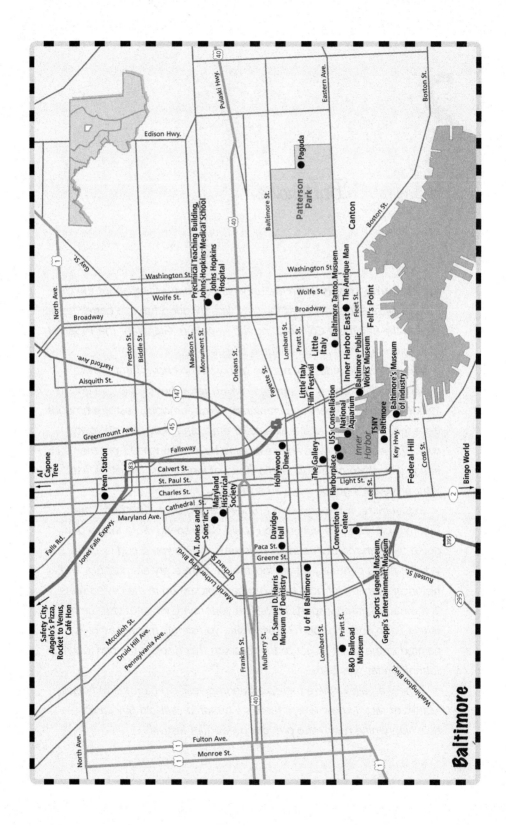

Pulaski Hwy.
40
Eastern Ave.
Boston St.
Edison Hwy.
Pagoda
Patterson Park
Baltimore St.
Canton
Boston St.
Washington St.
Washington St.
Wolfe St.
Wolfe St.
Gay St.
North Ave.
Broadway
Broadway
Baltimore Tattoo Museum
The Antique Man
Fleet St.
Preclinical Teaching Building,
Johns Hopkins Medical School
Johns Hopkins Hospital
Inner Harbor East
Fell's Point
40
Preston St.
Biddle St.
Madison St.
Monument St.
Orleans St.
Lombard St.
Pratt St.
Little Italy
Little Italy
Harford Ave.
Aisquith St.
147
Fayette St.
Little Italy Film Festival
Baltimore Public Works Museum
Greenmount Ave.
45
National Aquarium
USS Constellation
Baltimore
Baltimore's Museum of Industry
Fallsway
Inner Harbor
TSNY
Fallsway
Hollywood Diner
The Gallery
Penn Station
83
Calvert St.
St. Paul St.
Charles St.
Cathedral St.
Harborplace
Key Hwy.
Federal Hill
Cross St.
Al Capone Tree
Light St.
Lee St.
2
Bingo World
Maryland Historical Society
Maryland Ave.
A.T. Jones and Sons Inc.
Falls Rd.
Jones Falls Expwy.
Davidge Hall
Convention Center
395
Paca St.
Greene St.
Orchard St.
Martin Luther King Blvd.
Russell St.
Safety City, Angelo's Pizza, Rocket to Venus, Café Hon
Mcculloh St.
Druid Hill Ave.
Pennsylvania Ave.
Franklin St.
Mulberry St.
Dr. Samuel D. Harris Museum of Dentistry
U of M Baltimore
Lombard St.
Pratt St.
Sports Legend Museum, Geppi's Entertainment Museum
295
B&O Railroad Museum
Washington Blvd.
North Ave.
Fulton Ave.
40
1
Monroe St.
1

Baltimore

The holy grail of Baltimore curiosities? Selecting one would stir up a good debate, that's for sure. Picture a table of locals talking it over, each clutching a can of Natty Boh beer. (What, you never heard of Natty Boh? That's Baltimore shorthand for National Bohemian, a brand whose headquarters moved away. The beer stuck around.) If I were at that table, I'd nominate the giant ball of string. It has everything Baltimore seems to love: It came from a place that's gone, people liked it when it was there, and it's been reborn.

I'm also certain that our table would be full. That's because folks in Baltimore take a keen interest in their quirks. You might even call it ownership. One guy told me to call him, any time, day or night, if I had questions on any of the quirky tips he'd fed me—and he meant it. Another man, whom I expected to interview about the history of Fell's Point (which the redcoats considered a den of pirates), arrived with a stack of curious news clippings dating back more than a decade. "I've been waiting for you," my source quipped. My mouth dropped, and I apologize to all of you because there was no way I could pursue them all. From another source: "Now, what have you done about John Waters?"

And then there were sources right in my own family who really delivered. One, when reading this manuscript, made a critical correction. "The Buddy Dean Show wasn't 'a' Baltimore teen dance program," he said. "It was THE Baltimore teen dance program." That tidbit was bested only by a late elder, who wrote the Rosetta Stone of the local lingo known as "Baltimorese."

Curious? Read on.

Vision Quests

Down in North Carolina, a farmer with time on his hands, spare metal parts, and an abiding interest in wind power built the giant red, white, and blue whirligig now churning 55 feet above the American Visionary Art Museum. Turns out Vollis Simpson, the farmer-turned-artist, made his first whirligig on Saipan, where he was stationed during World War II. It powered a washing machine.

Count on the artists to be as interesting as their artwork at the ever-fascinating American Visionary Art Museum, a repository for our nation's unbridled creative doers who, generally speaking, make art just because they do.

Consider the Baltimore Glassman, as the late Paul Darmafall was known. Diagnosed with schizophrenia in his twenties, he figured out in his fifties that glitter and glass combine to make shimmering light. He then repaired to the woods near his Armistead Gardens home to make "signs" from his medium. "I cannot tell a lie," one begins. It portrays George Washington's face in glitter-glass.

After losing family members in a house fire, Missionary Mary L. Proctor—a self-proclaimed prophet from Tallahassee, Florida—started painting on doors. She did so at God's instruction. Her mosaic of Old Blue Willow plate shards, entitled *Grandma Old Blue Willow Plate*, depicts a child and her female elder: "I remember when I broke Grandmama [sic] old plates I thought she would whip me," reads hand-painted script on the piece. "Instead she hell [sic] my hands and said I forgive you cause just yesterday God forgave me and he said one must forgive to be forgiven."

Following a chain-saw accident at his North Carolina lumberyard, what did a recuperating Clyde Jones do? He chainsawed animals from logs. Temple Grandin, PhD, who is autistic and an associate professor at Colorado State University, thought long and hard about how to make slaughterhouses more humane. Her detailed plans for doing so were displayed (as was Jones's work) in a recent annual exhibit. Catch a new one every year.

A farmer's home-made whirligig has become a landmark outside the American Visionary Art Museum. SARA MORELL

In addition to the permanent collection, the museum at 800 Key Highway holds a themed annual exhibit. Call (410) 244-5858 or visit www.avam.org for details.

Move On, Dotty Org

Here comes Pokey, a PLATYPUS, pedaled by nine guys in white lab coats and red helmets. Pink tulle Fifi, a giant poodle, must be readjusting her paddle wheel in anticipation. For who can resist a Personal Long-Range All-Terrain Yacht Proven UnSafe?

It's Baltimore Kinetic Sculpture Race day, aka the East Coast Kinetic Sculpture Race Championship. Do you have a sculpture with moving parts that a human can propel 13 miles through the city? If so, c'mon down on the first Saturday in May. And don't forget the life jackets.

Fifteen-foot Fifi, a kinetic sculpture, enters the water during the annual Kinetic Sculpture Race through Baltimore's streets (and a bit of its harbor). DAVID KONE

"It does spark the imagination of those in the art field, but it also sparks those in the engineering field," says "Mother" Theresa Segreti, the race's queen bee.

Professionally known as Director of Art and Design at the American Visionary Art Museum, Segreti's the one whose lightbulb went off while watching *Good Morning America*. That's where she saw a race launched by Hobart Brown, the late California sculptor who came up with kinetic sculpture racing. This is not your typical right coast–type activity, but Baltimore was a great place to give it a shot. From two original vehicles in 1991—including Fifi, an example of what Segreti calls "pure craziness that doesn't make sense"—the race drew something closer to forty sculptures by 2008. With them came a phalanx of "kinetinauts," aka "the fearless artist engineers who build and pilot sculptures." "Kinetic chickens" volunteer to help run the race and "kinetic cops" ticket kinetic violators. Then there's the whole spectator ethic. Bring your boa.

Kinetic entrants can win in all kinds of categories, like the Golden Flipper for the most interesting water entry. Lately, the sculptures have been going into the harbor at Boston Street in the Canton area. One year, a *Titanic* on wheels entered the water, broke apart, and sank. Left behind? A rowboat full of kinetic participants.

The opening ceremonies start at 9:30 a.m., and folks watch for finishers between 3:00 and 4:30 p.m. If you're the type who needs a winter project, check out www.kineticbaltimore.com and start dreaming about your early-May race entry.

Cinema Paradiso

Next time you're in Little Italy, look up when you get to the formstone row house at the corner of Stiles and High. That's John Pente's place. The window on the third floor? That's where the projector sits for the popular Little Italy Open-Air Film Festival. It's the perfect height for the "screen" affixed to the building across the way.

Free films are shown Friday nights in July and August at 9:00 p.m.

The projector for Little Italy's Open-Air Film Festival resides in the third-floor bedroom window at the home of "Mr. John"—who has the best seats in the house. SARA MORELL

and draw upwards of 2,000 viewers. If you're in the neighborhood, don't miss it. Check the schedule at www.littleitalymd.com/openair.htm. The season always opens with *Moonstruck* (and the audience always recites with Cher: "Snap out of it!") and closes with *Cinema Paradiso*. In between, you might catch *Roman Holiday* or *Life Is Beautiful* or Baltimore-related films like the musical version of *Hairspray*. Music precedes the film, and free popcorn is passed around. I hear that free cannolis once made an appearance. Governors sometimes show up.

As for that screen and "Mr. John's" well-placed window, they're a serendipitous pairing. The screen was supposed to be a mural promoting Little Italy's restaurants, but it ended up branded a billboard by the city, sparking concern among residents about its future. So it sat up there overlooking the Da Mimmo Finest Italian Cuisine restaurant parking lot for awhile. Meantime, Mary Ann Cricchio, Da Mimmo's owner, happened to go to Sicily. One night she found herself in a piazza as an open-air movie was shown. Voila! The Baltimore neighborhood film fest was on its way after the Senator Theatre loaned a projector and Mr. John, now age ninety-nine, said they could use the third-floor room. After all, his son is sixty-nine—he doesn't need his old bedroom anymore.

Stealth, Secrets, and the Cemetery down the Block

When the College of Medicine of Maryland was built in 1812, it was thought that the soul continued to inhabit the human body after death. This made things tough for the doctors who were trying to bring science—in the form of human dissections—into the largely unregulated field of medicine. Against this backdrop, the college—known now as the University of Maryland's historic Davidge Hall at 522 West Lombard Street—was built to train doctors.

It's clear that the builders considered how to fashion a structure where secret dissections could take place. For instance, the building was located at what was then the edge of town and was surrounded by a high wall. Inside, clandestine stairways and doorways (perhaps even a trapdoor) led from the "anatomical theater," a lecture hall, to a secret dissection room guarded by faculty. To get there, or even find out about it, a student had to be invited.

Today the formerly secret room is the medical school's alumni association office. Although doorways now lead into the room, remnants of the secret passageways as well as the three sets of skylights remain. Visitors can tour the historic building—the nation's earliest medical education building still in use—and view a 2002 episode of the History Channel's *Secret Passages* Monday through Friday during normal business hours. You can also learn about Frank, a body-snatching janitor. After all, Westminster Cemetery, where Edgar Allan Poe is buried, is but two blocks away. The grave-robbing, all in the very legitimate service of science, went on until the early 1880s.

Sing your cavity blues away at the
National Museum of Dentistry.

Chop, Chop

See the world's most famous dentures appropriately located in a
museum that was the world's first dental school, established in 1840.
Yep, those are George Washington's fake choppers in that climate-
controlled Plexiglas case. They are not, as legend says, made of
wood—they're crafted from hippopotamus ivory. This is one of five
extant pieces of GW's dentures, displayed with reproductions of the
other four in the event you're looking for the full picture.

★ ★

The Dr. Samuel D. Harris National Museum of Dentistry at 31 South Green Street (410-706-0600; www.dentalmuseum.org) is the nation's repository for the history and care of teeth. In addition to George's phony pearly whites, you'll find the dental instruments used on Queen Victoria (whose dentist trained in Baltimore); the mouthpiece of one Penny Wilson, complete with lipstick traces, that helped this circus-style "iron jaw" performer pick up heavy stuff with her teeth; and an account of how fluoridation was tested in the child-heavy home of Robert F. Kennedy Jr. ("the device was found inefficient and difficult to maintain").

This is a great place to educate those who have yet to obtain their molars, but exhibits such as the Tooth Jukebox will draw their elders. It plays vintage toothpaste commercials that remind folks that "Ultra Brite gives your mouth . . . sex appeal!"

Ravin'

Mystery writer and poet Edgar Allan Poe is so closely identified with Baltimore that its pro football team is named after his famous poem "The Raven." Poe's father hailed from Baltimore. Edgar was born in Boston, Massachusetts, and raised in Richmond, Virginia, but he spent an important chapter of his life here. And he died here in 1849, reportedly under mysterious circumstances. Some say he was found in a gutter (and, he allegedly drank copious amounts at a Fell's Point bar, but that tale may be apocryphal).

Poe was buried in an unmarked grave in the family plot at Westminster Burying Ground. Over time, according to the Edgar Allan Poe Society of Baltimore, word got around that the bard's grave was not appropriately marked. A campaign was launched in 1865 to raise funds to do so. On November 17, 1865, the remains of Poe and his devoted aunt and mother-in-law (yes, she was both), Maria Clemm, were reinterred during a grand ceremony attended by no less than Walt Whitman. The remains of Poe's wife, Virginia, later joined them.

The "Poe Toaster" visits Edgar Allan Poe's
grave on the anniversary of Poe's death.

The large marble monument is located just inside the iron gates of the cemetery at the corner of Fayette and Greene, and it's open during daylight hours. Every January 19, the anniversary of Poe's birth, a stealthy stranger known as the "Poe Toaster" leaves the bard a bottle of cognac and three roses. In recent years, news stories allegedly unmasked this mysterious visitor. To be honest, we averted our eyes. Why ruin a good story? Meanwhile, the Poe House and Museum (www.eapoe.org/balt/poehse.htm) is nearby at 203 Amity Street.

Grand Slams

You don't have to be a sports fan to enjoy the memorabilia—and learn something—at the Sports Legends Museum at Camden Yards. To wit:

- J. Edgar Hoover was a huge fan of the Preakness, the Baltimore stop of horse racing's Triple Crown. The Woodlawn Vase, the race's elaborate silver trophy, was buried during the Civil War, which is probably the only reason it wasn't melted down for shot and/or spirited off to who knows where.
- The Baltimore Colts had the first professional cheerleaders in the National Football League, in 1954. (Take that, Dallas Cowboys!)
- I'd never heard of diehard local fan Wild Bill Hagy until I saw his picture here, leading the cheers from old Memorial Stadium's Section 34 like he did for years and years. Folks haven't forgotten him!
- The actual numbers unfurled from the B&O Warehouse (the longest building east of the Mississippi) alongside the stadium the night that Maryland's own Cal Ripken Jr. played his record 2,131th consecutive game on September 6, 1995, can be seen at the museum.
- The bed where Johnny Unitas was born is also on display right here.

All of this sports ephemera and much, much more tell the tale of sports in Baltimore and Maryland. You'll find it in the former Camden Station, the 1856 terminus of the country's first commercial railroad, the Baltimore & Ohio Railroad. The address is 301 West Camden Street (410-727-1539; www.sportslegendsatcamdenyards.com). The museum is affiliated with the Babe Ruth Birthplace.

The Truth Is Marching On

On a dark night in 1984, the Baltimore Colts up and left town. Poof! One day they were here; the next day, they were gone.

To say the NFL franchise left behind a legion of angry fans is a vast understatement. The Baltimore Colts Marching Band was none too pleased either, but the band held one ace. Their blue-and-silver uniforms were at the dry cleaner's. So they donned their gear and played on. And on and on and on . . . For eleven whole years they played, at more than thirty NFL games, the Philadelphia Thanksgiving Day Parade, and the Pro Football Hall of Fame parade and game. And, yes, the repertoire included the Colts' fight song. To the band, this was a way to remind the world (or, at least, the NFL) that Baltimore was without a pro football team.

All that changed when the city's new team, the Baltimore Ravens, played their first game in 1996. The Colts Marching Band traded blue and silver for purple and gold, and stepped onto the field as the Baltimore Marching Ravens. They made music history in 2007 as the first NFL band to play in Macy's Thanksgiving Day Parade.

The band's president, John Ziemann, who started playing percussion with the outfit in 1962, led the musicians through the city's professional football drought and shared this story with me. Thank you, John. Online, click "Ravenstown" at www.baltimoreravens.com.

Out of Right Field

Babe Ruth's father was a saloon keeper, and his bar was once located in a spot where present-day Oriole Park at Camden Yards now stands. In fact, it was situated between where second and third bases are today. Fitting, isn't it?

The Sultan of Swat was born three short blocks away at 216 Emory Street, now the Babe Ruth Birthplace Museum (410-727-1539; www .baberuthmuseum.com). Odd as it may sound, the Babe was born in this row house precisely because his daddy owned a bar. The family lived above the bar, but Mrs. Ruth wanted her child to be born in a more suitable environment. So, she went over to her parents' place on Emory Street. It was February 6, 1895, and only 11 degrees the day George Herman Ruth Jr. debuted.

Come see the actual room where this momentous occasion took place, now re-created in historic fashion. Also here: a bat given to the young ballplayer by Shoeless Joe Jackson, the Great Bambino's rookie baseball card from the 1914 Baltimore Orioles, and his hymnal from St. Mary's Industrial School. That's where the senior Ruths sent him when Babe's behavior took a nosedive, a reflection, perhaps, of the rough neighborhood. That's also where he really learned to play baseball. The rest, as they say, is history, and you can learn all about it right here.

Babe Ruth was born in this house.

★ ★

Youth and Just Us, the American Way

Few escape their past at Geppi's Entertainment Museum. Even the *Toy Story* generation—who are what, college-aged by now?—get their childhood memory buttons pushed at this pop-culture museum on the second floor of historic Camden Station at 301 West Camden Street (410-625-7060; www.geppismuseum.com). It's upstairs from the Sports Legends Museum.

Exhibits date to the late nineteenth century, but forget about the fossils. We're talking comic books, early marketing to kids, and evolving media. It's stuff that couldn't be more current.

Superstars in the comics collection begin with Superman's world-wide debut in Action Comics #1, circa 1938. "At the time," says curator Dr. Arnold T. Blumberg, "Superman couldn't fly but he could leap buildings in a single bound." Baby steps, folks, baby steps. Soon came Batman in 1939, who debuted via Detective Comics #27, then Captain America, who first showed up nine months before Pearl Harbor, in March 1941. The cover shows him punching out his era's worst villain, Hitler.

The first of the marketeers with their eye on the kid business created Palmer Cox's Brownies, circa 1883. These were spritely creatures based on different jobs, like policeman or sailor, or cultures, such as Irish or Chinese. They taught children good morals and appeared in books, puzzles, games . . . and even candlestick holders. (Guess they still used a lot of candles back then.) Over the years came all the rest: the Yellow Kid, Mickey Mouse, Spider-Man, and GI Joe. Rock and roll. Pez dispensers. There was a *Miami Vice* board game?

True story: Once, a guy well into his fifties approached the museum's curator in tears. He'd just seen a Hopalong Cassidy gun and holster set exactly like the one he'd had as a kid.

Baltimore entrepreneur Steve Geppi personally collected most of these pop-culture items. He's well-known for his Diamond Comic Distributors, Inc., for which fans of the early comics displayed here will no doubt want to thank him.

Like the Sweet Song of a Choir

That's alright, mama, if you've never seen an Elvis impersonator. Now may be your chance, though, because any red-blooded American should attend something called Night of 100 ELVISes at least once.

Bite into a fried peanut butter and banana sandwich and catch a surf-guitar version of "Love Me Tender" at this extravaganza, which is far more than guys in white jumpsuits. On three stages over two nights, at least twelve Elvis entertainers alternate ten-minute sets with any type of band you can think of. Break-dancers may fly to a remix of "A Little Less Conversation." Sounds cool, no?

Even cooler: You won't hear one Elvis song repeated on either night on one of three stages, called the Ballroom stage. However, professional Elvis Tribute Artists (aka ETAs), may have signature material. It's not uncommon for more than one to sing the same songs in their acts, according to event organizer Carole Carroll.

The faithful gather at the grand old Lithuanian Hall for the fund-raiser, which is always held the first weekend of December. Fans in tall hair or pink bowling shirts circulate through the Jungle Room, the Lounge, and the Ballroom (where you can get reserved tables) while grazing on a buffet of The King's favorites. In addition to the aforementioned PB and B sandwiches, the menu includes fried chicken, lil' ol' cheeseburgers, or green beans that haven't lost the bacon. And since this is Chesapeake Country, oyster shuckers are in the house. (And since this is the Lithuanian Hall, tiny cups of a native honey elixir called *viryta* are sipped.)

"A group of guys come dressed as Roman Gladiator Elvis," said Carroll. "One year, five guys in jumpsuits and five Priscilla look-alikes came from New York."

I gotta see this. It sounds like a scene. The event is so organized, it even coordinates a shuttle from two downtown hotels. To find out all the details, check www.nightof100elvises.com. Well, all the details but one, which I've always wondered about and finally had the opportunity to ask: What's the draw for Elvis impersonators?

"I'll tell you what most of them tell me," replied Carroll. "The girls."

A produce-piled wagon, piloted by one of Baltimore's dwindling number of "Arabbers," takes to the street.
SARA MORELL

Watermelon, Red to the Rind

If you see a guy leading a dressed-up horse pulling a produce-laden wagon, you've spotted a genuine arabber.

A what?

Yes, an arabber (pronounced AY-rabber), a last-gasp itinerant entrepreneur from an eighteenth-century way of life. The name apparently stems from the term "street arab," which means (I think) a homeless person (or something like that). I asked around and still haven't pinned down precisely why arabbers are called arabbers. That's just the way it's always been.

A dwindling breed, arabbers gather on Friday afternoons at the Carlton Street stables in West Baltimore. There, off an alley, they load up and head out. The hundred-year-old brick stable, with hand-scrawled signs and a spare dog, dates to horse-and-buggy days. Across the alley on the day I visited, a couple of retired arabbers, nicknamed China and Rio (they all used to have nicknames), helped load the wood wagon with artfully displayed mangoes, pineapples, greens, and other *Gourmet* magazine–looking fruits and veggies.

A third arabber was headed to a retirement home, where customers were waiting for him. He doesn't "sing" like the arabbers did back in the day, when dozens hit the streets. "Red to the rind, red to the rind!" you'd hear 'em call about the watermelon. And produce is no longer brought to Baltimore by boats delivering from Eastern Shore farms as it once was. Now, it's bought from a typical modern wholesaler. Still, some things just don't change. As always, the green arabbing cart rolls on red wheels made by Amish wheelwrights in Pennsylvania Dutch country, which is not that far away. The horse wears a fancy Baltimore harness with white bone rings, the same as the horses always have worn.

And the customers still await.

Another arabbing barn is in temporary quarters near the B&O Railroad Museum, and there's an arabbing center at 1102 North Fremont Avenue. Word has it that it may become a living-history museum. The Arabber Preservation Society maintains a Web site at www.baltimore md.com/arabber.

Pamplona for Pigs

The Running of the Pigs has neither the fired-up animals nor the gored runners of Pamplona.

No, the humble pigs arrive in their namesake "Pigtown" from a nearby farm. They're in this southwest Baltimore neighborhood strictly for a quirky and placid porcine salute to the nineteenth century, when these streets were semirural. Back then, the pigs came via railroad. Once in town, they were herded to slaughter from the nearby B&O Railroad Roundhouse (now the B&O Railroad Museum) and Union Stockyards through the working-class neighborhood. As the story goes, the locals turned out to cheer—and also to nab dinner.

The present-day "running" is part of the annual Pigtown Festival, held in early September (www.pigtownfestival.com).

"They're market size," reports Don Phillips of Citizens of Pigtown. He grew up on a Minnesota pig farm but never butchered one until he was a Peace Corps volunteer in the former Soviet Union. With those credentials, he knows what a market-size pig weighs. For the record: 220 to 280 pounds.

Along a 20- to 30-yard portion of Washington Boulevard, a handful of pigs—say, four—trot from a corral to the running's "finish line" and back, accompanied by local luminaries, including their farmer and Pigtown's costumed mascot. Along the way, local kids learn porcine trivia, like the fact that pigs have no sweat glands. That's why they roll in the mud.

A Stable for Iron Horses

A handsome 1856 locomotive featured in 1999's *Wild Wild West* and 2003's *Gods and Generals* resides at the Baltimore & Ohio Railroad Museum, the Cary Grant of the rail yard. But that's not the former roundhouse's best curiosity. Here at 901 West Pratt Street the best curiosity will be yours, sparked by what you learn about how the B&O helped to build the state and, by extension, the nation. It sounds a little corny, but it's true.

The Western Hemisphere's first commercial railroad started right here in 1827. By the time the enterprise had picked up steam (no pun intended) in the mid-nineteenth century, the B&O gave the competing Chesapeake & Ohio Canal such a run for its money that the latter—the interstate highway of its time—folded. These two transit systems opened up what was then frontier.

The B&O's story is legend. It brought you the tale of "Tom Thumb," the first American-built steam locomotive that carried passengers at 13 miles an hour in 1830. It helped to birth long-distance communication, when, on May 24, 1844, Samuel F. B. Morse sent a telegraph message over its wires.

This good-looking 1856 specimen has been in numerous movies and resides in the world's oldest lomotive collection, found at the B&O Railroad Museum.

The roundhouse turntable, once used to repair locomotives, allows the museum to move its impressive collection of locomotives, such as its medieval-looking 1832 "grasshopper" with its spiky rods that move up and down. Numerous locomotives from more recent times are housed in an adjacent building.

We can thank the B&O's early interest in public relations for the museum's 150 pieces of major railroad equipment going back 175 years. A bunch of late nineteenth-century suits launched a campaign to lure customers to "ride the historic B&O." Luckily, the penny-pinchers over in accounting had retained the outdated technology, so what you see is the hemisphere's most important and comprehensive collection of American railroad artifacts.

For more information on the Baltimore & Ohio Railroad Museum, call (410) 752-2490 or visit www.borail.org.

Who's That Girl?

A would-be case of mistaken identity berths at the Inner Harbor. The USS *Constellation*—the last all-sail warship built by the U.S. Navy— arrived in Baltimore in 1955. Apparently, after an illustrious 150-year career, she was back home where she was built.

But she wasn't.

The *Constellation* that arrived was not the *Constellation* that was built here. Turns out there were two old sailing vessels named for Old Glory's stars. The first was broken up at a Portsmouth, Virginia, shipyard about the same time as the second USS *Constellation* was constructed. *She* is the ship you can tour at the Inner Harbor, a sloop of war that set sail in 1853. The definitive study that untangled her pedigree wasn't released until 1992.

Constructed of live-oak frames and still about 50 percent original, the USS *Constellation* is the nation's only active-duty Civil War ship still afloat. The captain's sleek stateroom, the officers' quarters, twenty-two cannons, sixty hammocks, and a hospital occupy her four decks. She's berthed at Pier 1 at 301 East Pratt Street (410-539-1797; www.con stellation.org).

However, just as Adam donated a rib to Eve, it is said that eight pieces of the first *Constellation* are built into *Constellation* #2. USS Constellation Museum director Chris Rowsom has thought long and hard about where those pieces might be. "It's a great thing if they are there, but we haven't been able to come up with a definitive location," he said. But if he had to guess? Check out the joinery in the cabins on the berth (i.e., third) deck.

Oh, and by the way, there's a third USS *Constellation*. Bet nobody confuses the retired aircraft carrier with an old square-rigger from the golden age of sail.

The nation's last active duty Civil War ship is docked at the Inner Harbor. SARA MORELL

Domino Aglow

An icon the size of a basketball court lights up the Inner Harbor. Topping the Domino Sugar Plant at 1100 Key Highway, the Domino Sugar sign can't be missed and reminds the world that this used to be a center of industry. The sugar-making continues and $100,000 per year reportedly keeps the sign's red lights glowing. Here's guessing the sailors coming into port and the residents of the harbor's new condos are all happy to see the sign blaze on.

Shiver Me Timbers

Yo ho ho, mateys. You'll need to wait until night to drink that bottle of rum, when the Pyrate Invasion begins. That's the evening portion of the twofold Pyrate Invasion–Privateer Day, an eye patch–filled celebration of Fell's Point's seafaring past held on a Saturday in mid-April.

Privateer Day is on deck during the daylight hours, the family-friendly portion of the day. And that makes sense because, after all, privateers were street (and sea) legal. During the nineteenth century, privateers lived in Fell's Point. They were sailing merchants of war who hit the high seas on behalf of the U.S. government, especially during the War of 1812. Back then, the U.S. Navy was small and needed reinforcements. The captains aboard Baltimore clippers built in Fell's Point are said to have done a jolly good job. So good, in fact, that the British considered the city's original port area to be a dangerous "nest of pirates."

A reenacted sea battle off Fell's Point has been added to Privateer Day's storytelling, costume contests, and other events, more about which can be found at www.fellspointdevelopment.com. No less a vessel than the *Pride of Baltimore II,* the city's seagoing tall ship, partook recently. By nightfall, the pirates and wenches take over the streets, which are well-known for a good mug o' grog. Drink and food specials at Fell's Point pubs and restaurants start about dinnertime.

Treasures and oddities abound at The Antique Man in Fell's Point.

A Four-Legged Chick and a Giant Ball of String

"This kind of stuff, for me, is fun," says Bob Gerber, The Antique Man, at 1806 Fleet Street. His store's been in Fell's Point since 1986.

Just look around his jam-packed shop, which includes plenty of old-fashioned antiques and is open only by appointment (410-732-0932) or from 1:00 to 5:00 p.m. on Saturdays and Sundays. There's a two-headed mummy in a glass case, a former sideshow attraction. ("I bought him from an old carnival guy in Glen Burnie about thirty years ago. Made in 1906," says Gerber.) Hanging in Gerber's office is a

colorful tribute to a muse of local filmmaker John Waters: "In Memory of Edith Massey, May 28, 1918–October 24, 1984." ("She had a little junk shop over on South Broadway.") A stuffed four-legged chick, now about seventy years old, stands on a shelf. ("He had brain and motor coordination; he ran like a dog.") Not far away is a 150-year-old shrunken head, a hand from a Freddie Kruger movie . . . and so on.

In the center of the shop, behind Elvis, sits the giant ball of string from the late, lamented Haussner's Restaurant, which operated for decades before closing in 1999. "I didn't want it to leave Baltimore," says Gerber. So, when the restaurant's effects went up for bid (including a Sotheby's auction of its significant nineteenth- and twentieth-century artworks), Gerber paid $8,900 for the fabled ball. It's made from string that once bundled restaurant linens. Why roll those into a ball? Don't ask me. It must be one of those Baltimore things.

Flashes of Artistry

Stripper Blaze Starr may have been the best-known performer along Baltimore's famously infamous Block, but Tattoo Charlie plied his trade here, too. This I learned at the Baltimore Tattoo Museum at 1534 Eastern Avenue (410-522-5800; www.baltimoretattoomuseum.net).

More tattoo parlor than museum, the museum part of the operation focuses on the masters of tattoo, their apprentices, and their designs. Like Tattoo Charlie. He worked in the days when an eagle on a serviceman's forearm more than sufficed. Now, the debate rages over whether tattoos are high art or craft. At the museum, you'll see the progression, from snakes and American flags to skulls and dragons. They're displayed as "flash," the old name for a page of these designs. There's also more detailed work, like Neptune with his sea horses.

Many designs speak for themselves, just as the museum's case of tattoo "guns," or "drills," or whatever they're called, speak for themselves. Once you see them, you'll know just what these tools do: They insert ink into your skin.

Duckpin bowling balls fit in the palm of your hand.

Strike, Sally, Strike

I'd always heard that duckpin bowling, the game with the palm-size bowling balls, was born in Baltimore. After rummaging around online, I'm not so sure anymore. But why mess with a good story? I've run into a yarn about how a few Babe Ruth–era Orioles came up with the name. I've also listened to a favorite Baltimore source talk about setting duckpins in his local neighborhood alley. Baltimore certainly claims its affinity with the sport.

Fewer neighborhood alleys exist than they once did, but you can still find some. Then there's Mustang Alley, an upscale operation that understands its city's roots. Originally, the restaurant/bowling alley's

plans involved twelve lanes of ten-pin only. But local heads prevailed, and four duckpin lanes were added to the mix. Turns out a guy in Pennsylvania leases the actual duckpins. That's how you get hold of them, reports Mustang owner Tim Koch, though replacement parts for the pin setters are tough to find.

Baltimoreans of a certain age like to stop in and reminisce. Some who once owned duckpin lanes come to see the machines operate again. It's easy to get the impression that duckpin devotees are a dying breed, but there's good news: The young crowd at Mustang Alley, between Little Italy and Fell's Point (1300 Bank Street; 410-522-2695), views the game as a fun novelty.

An Icon High above the City

What do Florence, Italy, and Baltimore, Maryland USA, have in common? Or, more to the point, the Palazzo Vecchio and heartburn?

Hmmm. Hard to say. But their harmonic convergence rises fifteen stories above Baltimore, courtesy of an early heartburn-headache remedy entrepreneur. Captain Isaac Emerson built the replica of the iconic palazzo tower alongside his early-twentieth-century Bromo-Seltzer plant downtown. The tower's presence (and history) is just curious enough to require our embrace, which, I can assure you, Baltimoreans have done for a century.

The Emerson Bromo-Seltzer Tower, now artists' studio space, was finished in 1911. At the time, it was the city's tallest building. A 51-foot Bromo-Seltzer bottle lit by 596 lights revolved atop the tower until 1936. Structural concerns brought the bottle down, but more modern renovators didn't forget its impact. An appropriate Bromo-Seltzer bottle cobalt-blue glow now shines from the tower's cupola at night. And the tower's four clock faces tick on, but instead of numbers, the clock faces spell out BROMO-SELTZER.

Do they even sell Bromo-Seltzer anymore? Remind me to check next time I'm at Rite-Aid.

Baltimore's iconic Bromo-Seltzer Tower, named for the headache remedy once made here.

Pump It Up

The Baltimore Public Works Museum faces facts. "Public works is the basic infrastructure upon which modern civilization rests," reads the introduction inside the front door. Who's gonna argue?

Here, under Plexiglas, rests a circa 1790 water drain made of white oak (which, incidentally, is the Maryland state tree). The simple trough once emptied water into the harbor near present-day Pratt and Light Streets.

★ ★

Black-and-white photos depict horse-drawn carts hauling garbage, a service that started in Baltimore in 1872. The carts are a far cry from the Bobcats and Load Packers—aka garbage trucks—of today. Did you know that 131 Load Packers serve present-day Baltimore? Or that 280 million glasses of water are consumed in Baltimore every day? It's true.

The museum is housed in the Eastern Avenue Pumping Station, an elegant 1912 brick building with a turret that's still used for public works. In fact, one-third of the city's wastewater circulates in the pumping station (not the museum, thank heavens). It's located at 751 Eastern Avenue near Pier 7 at the Inner Harbor (410-396-5565; www .publicworksmuseum.org). Don't miss the above and below streetscape outside, where you can stand next to a traffic signal and peer down at the sewer and water pipes that keep the city civilized.

Sowing Seeds

After he got out of Alcatraz, gangster Al Capone needed medical attention for an unsettling condition—syphilis. The board at Johns Hopkins apparently wouldn't accept him (or so I was told), so he went to Union Memorial Hospital at 201 East University Parkway with his "family," which included a food taster.

Appropriate care ensued. In appreciation for the hospital's help, Capone donated two weeping cherry trees to its grounds. One thrives so spectacularly that for Union Memorial's recent 150th celebration, the powers that be used the tree for a fund-raiser and commissioned an arborist to grow babies. Now, little "Al Capone trees" are out there dotting the Maryland landscape.

Slow and Steady

Back when your granddaddy was a glimmer in his mother's eye, the Johns Hopkins Medical School doorman kept pet turtles in a grassy area near the school. Why? It's just something Colonel Benjamin Frisby, doorman from 1889 to 1933, did. One day a gynecologist by the name of Kelly approached him about racing the turtles. Before you knew it, the med school's doctors and faculty gathered annually for a race at which betting is alleged to have taken place.

Then came the 1970s, and the faculty turned the race over to first-year medical and radiology students. Now, the Turtle Derby held the May Friday before the Preakness raises money to help sick kids. The race takes place in the courtyard of the Preclinical Teaching Building at 1830 East Monument Street near the corner of Wolfe Street. "Gamblers," aka families, can check out the competition in a turtle-size paddock.

Little modeling clay "flags" on straws humanely mark the racers, who are pitted against one another in heats with names like Mud Slider Marathon. Like their crustacean cousins once did in Crisfield at the annual crab derby (see the Crisfield entry in the Eastern Shore chapter), the turtles "race" out of a round track. "How do you get them to go straight?" was the rhetorical question posed by Patrice Brylske, director of Child Life Services, which is part of the Johns Hopkins Children's Center. Her department benefits from the race.

The seventy-seventh stakes was run in 2008. Annual pins promoting the race are gingerly stored in the Johns Hopkins Medicine Archives.

And you thought Hopkins was all serious medicine.

Needs New Feet

Need a Halloween getup? Go see George Goebel at A. T. Jones & Sons Inc., which has been supplying Baltimore's costuming consumers since 1868.

Mostly, the company creates costumes to outfit operas. When I visited, Goebel, who started working here in 1950, was brushing metallic paint onto a pair of boots belonging to Luminaire, the *Beauty and the Beast* character. In the back, stacked boxes of costumes awaited transport to an Ohio dinner theater. "There's *Carmen* over there," said Goebel. That was the following week's production priority at the 708 North Howard Street business, a century-old, three-story building the company moved into in 1955.

★ ★

Need a petticoat? Call A.T. Jones, the 140-year-old costumery in downtown Baltimore. SARA MORELL

Gray wool coats, tapestry gowns, gold petticoats, outfits with spinning plates affixed—costumes are hung, stacked, and stored everywhere at A. T. Jones. During a tour, Goebel gestured: "These are the Winkies." Across the corridor, a label read "Chain mail sleeves. Macbeth." Another box, labeled "Brown horse with white blaze. 1 person" had a note pinned to it: "Needs new feet." From a ceiling hung the head of the original Baltimore Oriole. Goebel created the mascot. (Ever wondered why the Oriole danced atop the dugout at old Memorial Stadium? It's because his feet were too big to run up and down the stairs.)

Artist A. T. Jones arrived in Baltimore before the Civil War and opened his costume shop soon after. "This was a show business town," says Goebel, who also has turned a magic trick or two in his time. After the business passed through three generations of Joneses, Goebel and his son bought it in 1972. The costume shop is open to the public by appointment by calling (410) 728-7087. The adjacent theatrical makeup store is open from 9:00 a.m. to 4:30 p.m. Monday through Friday.

Look Before Crossing

Safety City replicates Baltimore's Inner Harbor area downtown, and it's kid-size for a reason. It was built to teach local children safety in their city, whether they're out biking, walking, or wondering whether to open a fire hydrant on a hot summer day. So, Safety City, located in the middle of Druid Hill Park, looks like a place they recognize. Sorta. The swimming pool blue "Inner Harbor" is on the south side of

A mini downtown Baltimore located in Druid Hill Park teaches kids safety.

the mini-downtown. Fort McHenry is denoted by a flagpole set in a five-sided base, just like the fort's five sides. On the north side of the "harbor," kids will see a mini Legg Mason tower—just like the tower downtown.

The abbreviated city has shortened streets with striped white lines, a regular stoplight at an intersection, signs like KEEP RIGHT, a fire hydrant, and pedestrian crossing signals. There's even a strip of railroad track. Local schoolchildren attend sessions here from April until October. If you're out of elementary school and visiting Druid Hill Park at 2600 Madison Avenue, stop and see if Safety City is open. If not, you can call the park at (410) 545-6854. Or grab your tennis racquet, sit by the lake, go to the Maryland Zoo, or otherwise check out this 745-acre city park that dates to the 1860s.

Blue Screen Special

In 1982 Baltimore's own Barry Levinson wrote and directed *Diner,* a cinematic ode to his hometown. He found an abandoned diner in New Jersey that originally hailed from Long Island and had it shipped to Charm City. Since then, it has enjoyed a dual career as a movie set and training ground for students.

Now known as the Hollywood Diner, the classic silver eatery at 400 East Saratoga Street (410-962-5379) serves up breakfast and lunch, brought to you by students from the Chesapeake Center for Youth Development (CCYD) and their workforce training program.

From time to time, the diner returns to its Levinson-era roots, offering authenticity that only chrome counter stools can provide. Ivan Leshinsky, the executive director of the CCYD, recalled that the diner was also featured in Levinson's *Tin Men, Avalon,* and *Liberty Heights.* Actress Meg Ryan played a teary scene here in *Sleepless in Seattle,* in which the diner was fictitiously set in nearby Washington, D.C. Crews from *Homicide: Life on the Street* and *The Wire*—tales of this city inspired and/or created by David Simon, a former *Baltimore Sun* reporter—have also filmed here.

Hollywood Diner serves up movie memories, lessons for students, and a hearty meal.

Baltimore almost lost the diner to New Jersey in the early 1980s after *Diner* wrapped. As Leshinsky recalls, former Baltimore mayor (and later, Maryland governor), the colorful William Donald Schaefer, led the drive to bring the diner back. "He said we should make this as famous as the steps of the Philadelphia Art Museum in *Rocky*," Leshinsky says.

The State's Attic

The Maryland Historical Society, founded in 1844, houses state treasures such as the original manuscript of the "Star-Spangled Banner," penned by Marylander Francis Scott Key. A 1,700-pound fiberglass dog towers 14 feet above the building's Park Avenue entrance. That's Nipper, the old RCA (and before that, RCA Victor) icon. Built in the 1950s by Baltimorean Howard Adler, Nipper once greeted travelers

from atop a building on the Baltimore-Washington Parkway. He's also a sign (well, at his size, maybe a knock on the head) that the grand old society's museum at 201 West Monument Street (410-685-3750; www.mdhs.org) holds more than dusty manuscripts.

Folks rummaging through an exhibit called "Nipper's Toyland: 200 Years of Children's Playthings" will find a Ouija board, invented in Baltimore in 1925. Jolly King Gambrinus, a sizable soul, holds court in his own nook near the museum entryway. This is his latest niche; his first was above a door at the John Frederick Wiessner and Sons brewery on North Gay Street back in the nineteenth century. The king, restored in the 1960s by a brewery truck mechanic, is the earliest surviving zinc sculpture of this particular local pop icon.

Here also you'll find Marylander Eubie Blake's horn-rimmed eyeglasses, near the jewels once owned by the "Queen of Rome." In case the name doesn't ring a bell, she was Baltimore belle Betsy Patterson, whose brief marriage to Jerome Bonaparte was voided by his brother, Napoleon. She refused to forsake her "rightful title," and retired to Baltimore's Mount Vernon Square to live out her days in the style to which she had become accustomed.

Gettin' Medieval

Sculptor Tim Scofield's flying machine looks trapped in time. Did it catapult fire over castle walls, or rocks into Roman lion pits?

Its working fulcrum and axis, which render the flying machine functional, derive from the Stone Age. When Scofield straps on his black vest (made from the same stuff as the bulletproof ones), which has hooks to bind him to his functional sculpture, it looks like he could do battle in the Spanish Inquisition.

Up, up, and away! Good old Charles Atlas–era free weights counterbalance the weight of the strapped-in flyer. Scofield's invention is tethered to the ground. The machine pivots over then back, and rotates all around. Its aerialist, meantime, floats in slo-mo, as if trapped

A sculptor and friend take flight on his invention. JOSHUA GILLELAN

in Jell-O. According to another seasoned aerialist, it's important to land on your hands and feet.

"I made it in order to experience flight," says Scofield, who, when last we spoke, was plotting his next daredevil extravaganza in metal.

Keep an eye out for Scofield and his flying machine at local arts events, such as Baltimore's huge summer ArtScape festival in mid-July (www.artscape.org).

Mystical Pizza

Not only is Baltimore full of curiosities, they wave their arms and shout, "Hey, over here!" Take the Big Slice at Angelo's Pizza & Carry Out at 3600 Keswick Road (410-235-2595).

It was a hot and sticky June afternoon. Heat rose from the asphalt at Safety City in Druid Hill Park. Source of my day's caloric intake? Coffee. So, armed with directions from a local, I headed to a nearby lunch place for a real meal.

Alas, I missed the turn and ended up in the Hampden neighborhood. I parked and walked into a pizza and sub joint. Easy in, easy out, I figured—and probably pretty cheap. Inside, a notice was scrawled and posted at the counter: No slices on Fridays after 4:00 p.m. A slice of pizza! That *is* quick, easy, and cheap. I ordered one.

A foil-wrapped package the size of my Toshiba laptop arrived. This is a pizza slice? I unwrapped it. Awed, I photographed it. Then I ate it. Mmmmm! The crust was papery thin. I introduced myself to the owner and told him I believed I had found another Maryland curiosity. Then he told me his last name: "Pizza."

You can't make this stuff up.

Really Out There

Did you hear the one about the guy who bought the house, in Hampden, complete with a garage? The guy's working in his restaurant one day, and an old customer comes in. Says he heard about the new house. "Then he told me that in that garage in the twenties, a couple of guys built a rocket and tried to launch it to Venus," says home owner Geoff Danek.

The tale, backed by an article supplied by the customer, launched Danek on his own journey to find out more. Turns out that three amateur scientists put eight months and nearly $5,000 into a 24-foot rocket covered with varnished sailcloth. One of the trio, Robert Condit, climbed aboard one August day with fifty gallons of gas and no solid

A failed 1920s expedition to Venus inspired a Hampden restaurant's name.

plan for how he'd get back from space. Luckily, he didn't need one. The shakedown flight never got off the ground, and Condit was last seen headed for Florida.

Danek's quest to learn the fate of the faux astronauts hasn't been much more successful than the launch, but maybe that doesn't matter. Along the way, Danek (who owns the eatery Holy Frijoles) and partner Brian Carey bought one of Hampden's old, smoky bars and turned it into a restaurant. He was also struck by divine inspiration. Standing over a rocket—a 1950s amusement park ride—at an Annapolis yard

★ ★

sale one day, the name of the new restaurant became clear. Rocket to Venus, at 3660 Chestnut Avenue (410-235-7887; www.rockettovenus .com, where you can read the full tale of Condit and friends) now sports the amusement park rocket on the outside and a retro-modern interior with portholes, copper, and aluminum. It's said the roasted Brussels sprouts ain't half bad either.

It's a Café, Hon

In lots of places, "hon" is a term of endearment. It is in Baltimore, too. But "hon" also has morphed into a noun that describes a certain type of woman. These are the working-class ladies who call you "hon" when they take your order or stamp your ticket. Back in the day, they wore beehive hairdos and cat's-eye glasses.

Café Hon, a Baltimore icon in the Hampden neighborhood.

Paramours and Zincs

Let's talk. About this Baltimore working-class accent thingy, in which folks refer to the city as "Bawlamer," Maryland as "Murlin," sink as "zinc," and, of course, call one another "hon"? If you get online, you'll easily read all about it.

Well, you've got your sources and I've got mine. I depend on the *Oxford English Dictionary* of Baltimorese, the pamphlet entitled "A Fairly Compleat Lexicon of Baltimorese," released in 1960. *Baltimore Sun* writer John Goodspeed wrote a column called Mr. Peep's Diary, and authored this clever work. I understand it's the first compilation of Baltimorese (also known as "Bawlmerese," among other spellings) and it's hard to find. Lucky me, I had no trouble. John's widow is my mother-in-law, Anne.

John, who lived to be eighty-six, always told the story in his native Texas accent about arriving in Baltimore from Fort Worth in the 1940s, finding a Baltimore rooming house, and wondering why on earth his new landlady was talking about a "zinc." Here are some of his other takes on how to pronounce the local language, recorded in his fairly compleat lexicon:

arnjoos = orange juice; authoritis = arthritis; bobwar = barbed wire; booern = born; chowld = child; dewer = door; fahr = fire; iggle = eagle; kooer = car; melhawk = mohawk; moran = meringue; oorning = awning; owen = on; padder = powder; and, oh, that's enough! Except samidge = sandwich and, of course, zinc = sink.

I also remember hearing John talk about the "paramour." Can you guess what it is? Here's a hint: Fetch it from your garage and mow your lawn. Yea, you got it: the *power* mower!

Which brings us to Café Hon, located in the one-time working-class Hampden neighborhood on "The Avenue," aka 36th Street (1002 West 36th Street; 410-243-1230; http://cafehon.com). The Hon Bar is right next door. Look for the giant pink flamingo on the building's facade. There's no way on earth you can miss it.

Established in 1992, Café Hon got its name when owner Denise Whiting's buddy asked her what she planned to call her new venture. "It's a café, hon," she replied. That name didn't quite roll off the tongue, ergo the abbreviated version. Set in an 1874 building that once housed a hardware store, the café brings you 1950s-era comfort food like pies, egg salad on cheese toast, and "Much Better than Mom's" meat loaf. That said, the menu isn't calcified in the past. The lunch menu features items such as a hummus powerhouse sandwich. Present-day folks need to live modern lives, hon.

Miracles Grow

Those not in the know can watch *Miracle on 34th Street* play for the umpteenth time on TV. Those in the know crowd the other Miracle on 34th Street. It's at the edge of the Hampden district, and it is one serious Christmas miracle. Residents on two sides of one block slather their homes in holiday decorations and lights, enough to make the Grinch smile.

> *They've got Mickey and Snoopy and Santa and Angels.*
> *Candy canes, gingerbread, white doves, and mangers.*
> *And overhead of it all*
> *Strings of lights that are two stories tall . . .*

OK, Rudolph may or may not fly through here, but if he does, he'll need to nod to Whos in Whoville, a snowman made from a bicycle wheel, and Natty Boh angels—yes, angels made from National Bohemian beer cans, Baltimore's favorite. Artist and resident Jim Pollock made these purely Baltimore pieces. During the holiday extravaganza on his block, tucked between Keswick and Chestnut, Pollock also puts together a gallery in his front room: snowflakes painted on the floor, Santa crabs. The block's big hubcap Christmas tree is in his front yard.

"Some people move to this block just to participate, and some move to this block and pretend they don't know what's going to happen," he quipped.

According to the "Miracle" Web site, www.christmasstreet.com, the street has been dispending its brand of holiday cheer for more than seventy years. The local media show up. Folks talk. How the heck can you move here and not know what's going to happen come holiday time?

Beehives and Housecoats

Don't have a beehive hairdo? Girlfriend—I mean, hon—I know where you can get one.

C'mon down to The Avenue in Hampden the second weekend in June. They've set up a beauty salon in the street and everything. It's HonFest!

What started as a backyard beauty contest behind Café Hon on 36th Street, aka "The Avenue," in 1994 has grown into a two-day neighborhood extravaganza drawing 50,000 folks that you can learn all about at www.honfest.net. Here's your chance to celebrate the era of the working-class "hons" of Baltimore, the gals who made industrial Baltimore so Bawlamer and have a little fun in a neighborhood that's now going a bit upscale.

The fest hasn't forgotten the beauty contest. Bands like the Hormone Replacements play in the street on Saturday while Baltimore's Best Hon contest takes place. As the motto goes: "The higher the hair, the closer to God!" Three age groups compete, starting with the little ones and their adolescent sisters ("Miss Honette"). Ten finalists from the grown-up division compete for Baltimore's Best Hon on Sunday. And here's where things go undeniably authentic: Not only must they

★ ★

Get your beehive and grab your cat's eye glasses for Hon-Fest. SARA MORELL

demonstrate a command of "Baltimorese," but an original dancer from the *Buddy Dean Show,* the local 1950s teen dance program (see John Waters's *Hairspray* for details), choreographs a dance for the finalists. They do the "honey hop," based on the bunny hop.

Did I mention that Sunday starts with the "HonFest Anthem"?

Baltimore's Best Hon of 2008 was a seventy-something retired nurse. The morning of the contest, she stood in her housecoat with a scarf wrapped around her head, and protested to her daughter that she wasn't dressed for the occasion. "Mom, you're dressed just fine," she replied, according to contest organizer Denise Whiting, Café Hon's owner.

The Pagoda

A grand old observation tower stands atop Hampstead Hill in Patterson Park. It's known as The Pagoda, and in true Victorian style, it's ornate. In true twenty-first-century style, we wonder: What the heck is that ornate Asian-looking pagoda doing in East Baltimore?

The four-story structure was designed and built during 1890–91 for a whopping $18,875. The design came from city parks superintendent

The Pagoda, an old Baltimore icon, stands in Patterson Park. SARA MORELL

★ ★

Charles H. Latrobe, and with a name like that, you've got to wonder if he had designing in his blood (Benjamin Latrobe being a major early U.S. architect who spent a bit of time in town). The 60-foot-high octagonal tower has undergone a couple of renovations during its long life. Stained glass studs the top of the Palladian-style windows, and a circular staircase takes you to the top, where the city's landscape, including the harbor, spreads out.

The Pagoda is open on Sundays from May through October from noon to 6:00 p.m., or call (410) 276-3676 to make other arrangements. Check www.pattersonpark.com.

You Can See Out . . .

A legendary Charm City tradition still visible—if you know where to look —in its native southeast Baltimore habitat stems from a very practical pre-AC consideration: "You see out. No one sees in."

That's what you get when you live behind painted window screens, and that's what you read on the back of the T-shirts for the Painted Screen Society (www.paintedscreens.org), the folks trying to preserve this quirky art form. From what I understand, screen painters use a specific technique to paint screens just right. Otherwise, from inside, a splotch of paint may look like a squished fly.

You can't argue with meticulous craftsmanship.

A Czech immigrant who painted fruits and veggies on his grocery's screen door in 1913 is credited with launching this Baltimore art form. William Octavek had creative aspirations: He later left produce to open an art store and pioneer screen painting. His recurring motif, which has been passed on, is based on a pastoral scene featuring a red-roofed

Bottletown, USA

If you hit the bottle at the Baltimore Bottle Show, somebody's gonna get upset. Especially if it's a bitters bottle. Those babies are worth some bucks.

Bitters bottles, milk bottles, pharmacy bottles, whiskey bottles—the world is full of bottles, and many of their ilk converge at the world's largest one-day bottle show. Usually held the first Sunday in March, the show draws dealers from the United States, United Kingdom, Germany, and Canada. To find out more about it, go to www.baltimorebottleclub.org/show.htm.

cottage. If you walk his old Highlandtown neighborhood streets, you'll understand his aesthetic. Block after block of row houses with white marble steps (another famous architectural detail of Baltimore) march down cement sidewalks; there are no trees and no lawns. A pastoral scene is just the antidote.

Old-style screen painting is fading. Dee Harget, who started painting in the 1960s, continues to break out her brushes for clients and can be reached via www.screenpainter.com. "There is a knack," she said. "Screen art is a cottage—red roofed. The red roof gives tribute to Octavek. Or a country scene, a mountain and lake in moonlight. It has to be serene, calming, and relaxing."

The easiest places to see screens are on the windows of the Hatton Senior Center, located at 2825 Fait Avenue, and on display at the American Visionary Art Museum (see the first entry in this chapter). Also, keep an eye out for *The Screen Painters* documentary, occasionally shown on TV and in theaters.

Baltimore's Half Boy

East Baltimore sideshow performer Johnny Eck was born without legs and has been dead nearly twenty years. But that hasn't stopped folks from talking. Around Baltimore, I kept hearing about him, first from The Antique Man in Fell's Point, who told me that he used to have some Johnny Eck memorabilia but sold it to a guy named Jeff, who works in the movies.

Jeff, as it turns out, has erected an online museum to Johnny and his twin, Robert. At www.johnnyeckmuseum.com you can read all about the "half boy" and how he became a sideshow performer, magician, and artist. That's how I tracked down Jeff, aka Jeffrey Pratt Gordon, a Baltimore-based movie professional (he wears a few hats in the business, but that's another story) who has plans for a museum in Johnny's former home at 622 North Milton Avenue. As he waits for neighborhood improvements, Jeff compiles permits and even a Baltimore city landmark designation for the house.

The Eck home sports Baltimore-style marble steps, where Johnny used to hold court. Johnny, who walked on his hands, starred in the 1932 cult classic *Freaks* and performed with his brother in a variety of shows, including Robert Ripley's *Odditorium*.

It's no surprise that the duo hailed from East Baltimore, where quirky seems to be a celebrated norm. (This is, after all, where residents create actual window displays, "nativity for all seasons," as Jeff himself calls them.) Jeff became an Eck fan while researching human oddities, an interest that grew from a college senior art project on freak potatoes. "They're ostracized—like human oddities," he said, "and I went down that path."

Meanwhile, I encountered Johnny's name again at the twentieth-anniversary screening of the documentary *The Screen Painters*. A guy in the audience grew up with him. Plus, Johnny himself is in the film. Among his accomplishments during his eighty years, he was a screen painter.

The show's sponsor, the Baltimore Antique Bottle Club, has been known to call their hometown "Bottletown." Considering the city's also known as Charm City, Mobtown, the City that Reads, Bawlamer, B'mo—and the hometown of John Waters and Blaze Starr—Bottletown adds a certain *je ne sais quoi,* don't you think?

Bottle collecting is serious stuff, with a variety of prices and specialties. Dr. William A. Andersen collects Baltimore bottles for their history. That's how he found out about Hopkins chalybeate. He read about it in an 1804 pharmacy publication. You make chalybeate by putting iron filings into wine, leaving it for two weeks, and then straining the filings. You then drink it. "I don't know what it did for or to you," he chuckled.

If you have a bottle you're curious about, bring it to the show for a free appraisal.

Derring-Do

Meathook or noodle? Left up to me, high on the trapeze, I'd go for the meathook. It sounds like it means business. A noodle? Not so much.

Students at the trapeze school along the Inner Harbor don't get to choose because the difference between a meathook and a noodle has nothing to do with their safety. Both are hooks used to fetch the hanging trapeze bar.

Folks come to TSNY Baltimore at 300 Key Highway (410-459-6839; www.baltimore.trapezeschool.com) from all over the Baltimore-D.C. metro area, even from the Virginia 'burbs. Maybe they're here for the workout. Or maybe they're beating that fear of heights. The workaholic D.C.-dwellers are probably looking to get an adrenaline kick from something besides a deadline.

A lesson starts with a "knee hang." It's just what it sounds like. A set split follows. It's a little scarier. Flyers literally do an upside-down split, prompted by a teacher. The lesson's final exercise is a catch, which means you finally get to play circus. The day I watched, most

★ ★

A high-flying student along the harbor takes advantage of the TSNY Baltimore trapeze school.

folks caught the hands of an instructor on another trapeze. This, according to participants, is the key adrenaline-pumper.

Did I mention flyers are rigged up to safety ropes? A safety net is strung as well, which is where the flyers land. That way, even students whose legs feel like noodles when they climb to the trapeze can summon the courage to fly into the friendly skies. A teacher stands by, for safety's sake.

Industrious Revolutionaries

A Baltimore pharmacist named Dr. Bunting invented Noxzema with the hopes it would ward off sunburn. One day a guy bought the stuff, took it home, and returned to announce, "You sure knocked out my eczema." With that, an iconic American product name was born.

The story of Noxzema and Baltimore's numerous other industrial firsts is told at the Baltimore Museum of Industry at 1415 Key Highway (410-727-4808; www.thebmi.org), in an area where warehouses, canneries, and other machinations of this city's working port once dominated. The world's first portable electric drill—with a hand grip—was invented here by a couple of guys named Black and Decker. They got the idea after working on a pistol for an outfit by the name of Colt.

In 1816 Rembrandt Peale, son of Colonial portraitist Charles Willson Peale, was running the Peale Museum in Baltimore. He began experimenting with a gas-powered "ring of lights" and invented the first gas streetlamps. Not only that, but he convinced a group of investors to back his invention. Baltimore soon lit up.

Umbrellas gained their commercial manufacturing foothold in Baltimore, and the first disposable standard bottle cap was invented here. The world's largest producer of drinking straws, Sweetheart Cup, toils away north of town in Owings Mills.

You have to admit, this intriguing city has more than its share of big-league firsts!

Great Wads of Money

Brooklyn

Technically, Bingo World is a Central Maryland curiosity because it's located—barely—across the border in Anne Arundel County. Spiritually, however, it's a Baltimore curiosity because, well, it just is.

Bingo World appears to be the largest commercial bingo hall in the entire country—apart from those at Native American casinos. The place is certainly something to see, with "videotab dispensers" ("Pirates of the Carib-bingo") popping and red lights flashing on one side of the hall, and tables lined up like a high school cafeteria on the other. This is where up to 2,000 people can play the day's three bingo games, including the 11:00 p.m. "night owl" session.

Today's bingo-players aren't shoving nickel-size divots across a bingo card like we did at summer camp. No, they're using fold-up

★ ★

techno-contraptions stored in cubbies and wired up so you can easily play multiple cards at once. "You'd be surprised how many people show up and say, 'If work calls, tell them I'm not here,'" said manager Dale Willey.

Folks have been playing bingo at 4901 Belle Grove Road (410-636-0311; www.bingoworld.com) for decades. In a way, it's a vestige of Southern Maryland's former life as a gambling mecca (and Maryland has recently voted to bring slot machines back to five locations). Busloads of folks come from as far off as New York to join Bingo World games, with Super Saturday jackpots that can reach $40,000. Bingo!

Bingo's gone techno in this giant commercial bingo hall just south of the Baltimore border.

3

Central Maryland

Combine equal parts *affluent Washington, D.C., and Baltimore sub-urbs, stir in rolling hills and scenic rivers, add lots of subdivisions, shopping centers, and one historic sailing town state capital. Voila! That's Central Maryland. The region's a Rorschach inkblot and a multiclass melting pot, spiced with a little of this, that, and the other thing.*

You can find a guy who collects old farm implements and one who collects Star Wars toys. The super-secret U.S. National Security Agency has collected some once super-secret stuff of its own, and put it on display at the National Cryptologic Museum.

Find a demolition derby north of Baltimore. West of the city, in formerly rural countryside, storybook characters from a former theme park now live on a farm.

Down in Annapolis, a distinguished-looking retiree puts on his jabot and hops aboard his Segway, while sailors burn their socks at the vernal equinox. You might even spot the governor over morning coffee in his reserved booth at a revered Annapolis deli before you amble across a short bridge to check out, yes, a "maritime republic," right here in the USA.

You just can't escape history in 'Naptown. The city stands where the Severn River flows into Chesapeake Bay, the nation's largest estuary. The bay started 12,000 years ago when glaciers melted and/or a meteor hit. No wonder there remains the legend of a mysterious resident creature of the deep . . . a tale that's faded, but hasn't quite died.

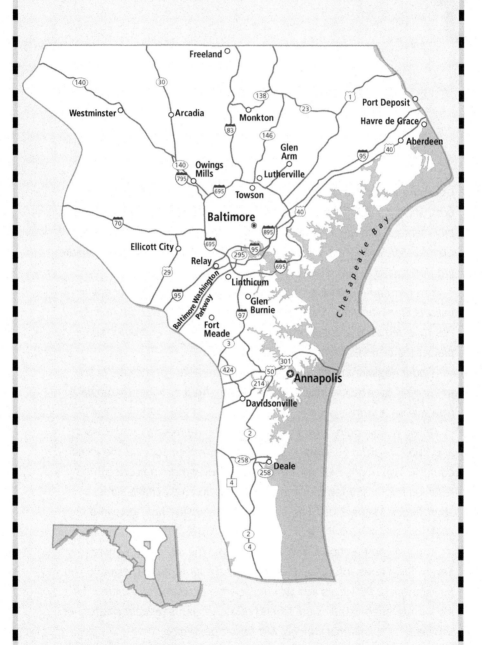

Freeland

140
30
138
23
1
Port Deposit

Westminster
Arcadia
83
Monkton
146
Havre de Grace
95
40
Aberdeen

Glen Arm

140
795
Owings Mills
Lutherville
Towson
695

Baltimore
40

Ellicott City
70
895

695
95
70

Relay
295
695

29
Linthicum

95
Glen Burnie
97
Fort Meade

Baltimore Washington Parkway

3

424
301
50
214
Annapolis

Davidsonville

2

258
258
Deale

4

2
4

Chesapeake Bay

Central Maryland

The Tanks Go Marching In
Aberdeen

Known far and wide as a "Mile of Tanks," they marched down the median strip at Aberdeen Proving Ground for nearly thirty-five years. But times change, and the hundreds of tanks and heavy artillery have backed away from the road.

An olive-drab U.S. M7 Priest, a Soviet T-34, and even a pink little Italian number (because you can't see pink at night) are among approximately sixty tanks lined up in precise rows outside the U.S. Army Ordnance Museum (www.ordmusfound.org), along with innumerable heavy artillery. An additional 240 artillery are situated throughout the base.

The collection dates to World War I. At that time, the United States had a good field gun, but couldn't produce them as fast as needed, according to Dr. William F. Atwater, the museum's retired director. So, a caliber board gathered artillery from all over the world and proceeded to catalog, test, and otherwise take a good, hard look at weapons developed by other countries. By World War II, the military was dissecting weapons for technical intelligence reasons. If you take apart a German Panzer 4 tank, maybe you can learn its battlefield weakness.

On the railroad tracks by the museum stands a particularly fearsome specimen. "Anzio Annie," formerly known as "Leopold," was one of the Germans' 11-inch (280-millimeter) K-5 railroad guns used during World War II. The monstrosity was adapted to run on rails. The gun saw action at Calais, France, when it shelled traffic in the English Channel, then at Anzio, Italy, where it shelled the Allies as they tried to break out of their beachhead. Anzio Annie took her toll. To see the big gun now, one of only two such known pieces of artillery, raises goose bumps.

★ ★

Cruisin' Ego Alley, a front row seat to the waterfront in Annapolis. JOE EVANS, PROPTALK MAGAZINE

A Hip Slip

Annapolis

At 70 feet wide and nearly 800 feet long, the "Market Slip" on your mariner's chart puts New York's fashion runways to shame. Come on down any warm-weather weekend, have a seat at centrally located City Dock, and see for yourself.

Here come the folks in big, buxom boats, often with a babe on the bow. Up and down they go, all day long. Muscles bulge. Occasionally, a good sailor shows up to impress onlookers by tacking in the tight space. Glory trails in his wake as he heads back out in the harbor from this hip slip of water lapping at the Historic District's heart. Locally, we call it Ego Alley.

"If you've spent the money, this is where you go show it off, whether it's a multimillion-dollar yacht, a $100,000 runabout, or a hand-built crabbing skiff," said Joe Evans, editor of *PropTalk*, a Chesapeake powerboating magazine.

With such a well-placed maritime stage, no one should be surprised by improvisation. Accidents happen. One former deckhand told me about the dunce who managed to jump both a boat and the dock, then knocked over a table at a waterside pub before coming to a stop. Annapolis Harbormaster Ric Dahlgren has chased down his share of folks who've dipped into the drink, intentionally or not. Once, a guy apparently fell in on a snowy night. "They found him hanging onto the back of his boat, frozen solid," Dahlgren said.

Then there was the time a disgruntled somebody, angered over an official decision, declared a "blockade" at the waterway's entrance. Dumb move. As Dahlgren points out, if there's one word you don't want to use when threatening maritime action, it's "blockade."

"When the boat got here, it was greeted by federal SWAT teams, DNR police, and Coast Guard response teams," Dahlgren said.

Ahem, mateys!

A Non-stick Wicket

Annapolis

Sports history boasts a cavalcade of epic rivalries: Frazier versus Ali, or the Redskins versus the Cowboys. And then there's the annual face-off between St. John's College and the U.S. Naval Academy.

No, it's not boxing or football. When these yin and yang institutions of higher learning meet on the court, croquet's the game. The annual April match looms large on Annapolis's calendar of events.

The first contest came in the early 1980s, after an adventurous Johnnie named Kevin Heyburn entered the academy yard and witnessed a ritual related to yet another epic rivalry: Navy's pep rally prior to the Army football game. Headed back to St. John's, which has no intercollegiate sports, he saw an academy official and mentioned how the two

★ ★

Mallet-wielding midshipmen take on neighboring
St. John's College students in Annapolis every spring.
COURTESY ST. JOHN'S COLLEGE; PHOTOGRAPHER, GARY PIERPOINT

schools had once been rivals. True, the commandant replied, but he didn't think St. John's should be challenging Navy to games these days.

Well, wouldn't you know, Heyburn got back to campus, remembered the croquet set in the library, and started asking around. One thing led to another, and soon St. John's issued a formal croquet challenge to the academy. The academy accepted.

Here's the thing: Although the two schools share a King George Street boundary, they didn't formally interact much back then. On the day of the first face-off, St. John's Board of Visitors & Governors member Admiral James Stockdale, on campus for a meeting, hit out the first ball. It was an auspicious start.

St. John's won that first year, and they have dominated the series ever since. Now, the match is about more than the croquet. It's a tradition. It's a spectacle. St. John's lawn fills with fans in picture hats or ties—family, alumni, and Annapolitans—enjoying what is usually a lovely spring day. This is one of the city's favorite parties, held the third weekend of April. For details, go to www.stjohnscollege.edu.

John Hancocks

Annapolis

Here's a fun fact: Annapolis is the only city in the entire country (well, of the original thirteen colonies) where the homes occupied by its state's signers of the Declaration of Independence still stand. You can visit all but one.

William Paca arrived to train in the law, was involved in Colonial politics, and was a member of the Continental Congress in his thirties. In 1782 he became Maryland's governor. His elegant Georgian mansion at 168 Prince George Street is operated by Historic Annapolis Foundation. For information, visit www.annapolis.org.

Charles Carroll of Carrollton lived here as a kid, left for a European education, and returned. Involved in a range of political activities, he also served in the Continental Congress. Carroll was the only Roman Catholic to sign the Declaration, and his house occupies an enviable waterfront

Birth of a Nation

If it hadn't been for a speech George Washington made at Maryland's State House, we all might be frog-marching behind a military dictator. Seriously.

After the Revolutionary War ended, Washington left New York and stopped in Annapolis just before Christmas 1783 to execute a key act in our nation's history. As the Continental Congress met, he resigned his commission as Army Commander-in-Chief in a room now known as the Old Senate Chamber. At a time when many expected Washington to become king, he instead returned his military authority to the congress. That act set the precedent that puts a civilian at the head of the United States military.

Washington's resignation speech is in the hands of the Maryland State Archives, which plans to display it at the Maryland State House, the oldest in continual use in the United States. Hardly a footnote in the Old Senate Chamber's history: As the congress met here between November 1783 and August 1784, it ratified the war-ending Treaty of Paris on January 14, 1784.

spot behind St. Mary's Catholic Church on Duke of Gloucester Street. More info can be found at www.charlescarrollhouse.com.

Samuel Chase, who earned the dubious distinction of being the only U.S. Supreme Court justice to be impeached (he was acquitted), trained in the law and settled here. He, too, served in the Continental Congress. His stately house stands at 22 Maryland Avenue, where it's a retirement home with limited touring hours. Call (410) 263-2723 for details.

Thomas Stone, of Charles County, also came to train for the law and lived in the Peggy Stewart House (also the name of a famous brig entangled in the era's tea politics, as mentioned in the Eastern Shore entry "A Spot of Tea"). He returned to his home for a time but came back to Annapolis in the 1780s. His three co-signers all lived in the city during the landmark year of 1776.

Just a Closer Walk with Thee
Annapolis

More than one witness at Middleton Tavern saw a pricey bottle of brandy float out of its top-shelf perch. Then the bottle hit the floor. Those in the know at the Colonial-era tavern probably shook their heads and chalked up the mess to Roland, one of this old port city's ghosts.

Keep an eye out, and ask questions. You'd be surprised what you learn about Annapolis ghosts. Legend says two brothers got drunk together ("probably at Middleton's," recounts Annapolis ghost-story expert Mike Carter, who shared these tales) and got into a fight over a woman. Long story short, one spread the word that his sibling had taken up life elsewhere when the second brother disappeared. Even agnostics must see that losing your head at your brother's hands might inhibit eternal rest. The headless ghost reportedly can be seen wandering around Green Street, St. Mary's Catholic Church, or the City Dock on starless nights.

Over on Pinkney Street, a woman may be in search of a warm bed at the city's old Shiplap House. It is said that a portrait painter, waiting for his wife to come to bed, heard footsteps on the stairs. The bedroom door opened, and the body settled next to him. She smelled of roses. "Are you wearing perfume?" he asked. She didn't respond. He felt her, and jeez, was she cold. When he flipped on the lights and looked over to where his lovely wife should have lain, he saw an indentation where a body had mussed the sheets.

These and other tales can be heard by those who join Carter on his Annapolis Ghost Tours. To order tickets, call (800) 979-3379 or visit www.ghostsofannapolis.com.

Mystery of the Deep

Loch Ness harbors "Nessie," and the alleged "Champ" emerges from Lake Champlain's deep. Here along the Chesapeake Bay, the legend of "Chessie" endures.

It's been awhile since the last Chessie sightings, but as recently as the 1980s the Smithsonian Institution bestowed a whiff of authenticity to the creature. Here's the evidence from the man who knows the most about such matters.

"I think it's a real thing," said longtime Maryland outdoors writer Bill Burton, who tracked Chessie sightings when he wrote for the *Baltimore Sun*. His opinion is in no small part due to the veracity of the witnesses he interviewed. Many who described Chessie to him are what he calls "trained observers"—Coast Guard officers, a Secret Service agent, an FBI man. "They're people who have no reason to come and say this, because they don't want the publicity," he said.

Here's what they usually saw: The sea monster's head was shaped like a football, and its neck was compared to a telephone pole. It was black to brown in color. No one could describe its eyes. Its movement tended to be up and down, not side to side like a snake.

In 1982 a Kent Island man videotaped the creature. At that time, interest was so hot that the Smithsonian looked into the situation. Their finding? "An unidentifiable animate object," Burton said.

As much as he's a believer, Burton can't hazard a guess as to Chessie's true identity. Speculation runs from a telephone pole in rough water to harbor seals passing through. Sightings came in from up and down the bay. One guy, fishing off Chesapeake Beach in early morning fog, noticed that the bluefish stopped breaking. "All the sudden, within 50 feet, he saw Chessie," Burton said. Which leads to one of his theories: The sightings stopped at a time bluefish populations declined in the bay. Whatever Chessie is or was, perhaps he (or she) was dining on bluefish.

What do you think?

Thomas Point Light, the last of its particular lighthouse species still found in its original habitat.

Nature's Way

Annapolis

Thomas Point Shoal Lighthouse sits like a crab out in Chesapeake Bay, the last of the bay's cottage-style screwpile lights left in its native habitat. It even remains an active aid to navigation, which means boat captains depend on it to light their way to a safe harbor.

Screwpile lights are structured to accommodate the bay's mushy, soft floor. Between 1854 and 1910, forty were built. Now, only four remain—and three of those have been moved alongside maritime

museums. The "cottage-style" designation means a dwelling is built atop the light's crablike pilings, the better to house Victorian-era lighthouse keepers. They occupied Thomas Point starting in 1875, when the light was built. Coast Guard guys did plenty of twentieth-century tours until automation arrived in 1986. On two floors are a kitchen, bathroom, and bedrooms, as well as modern weather-forecasting equipment. A consortium manages the light and offers docent-led tours departing from the Annapolis Maritime Museum (800-690-5080; www.thomaspointlighthouse.org).

Imagine how slowly time passes when you're stuck in a lighthouse because you've got to alert maritime traffic to potential problems, like fog. If you look down from the lighthouse railing, you'll spot names scratched into the rocky riprap that protects the light from waves. It must have been a slow day at Thomas Point shoal.

A high-visibility Maryland icon, the light is the subject of numerous photographs, paintings, Christmas ornaments, and so on. Look closely at the western side for something most voyeurs miss. Stuck to the building is a long, narrow box. If it were in the mountains, a crescent moon might be carved on the door. It's a straight 20-foot drop back to nature.

R.I.P.
Annapolis

John Paul Jones, a Scotsman with a hearty sense of derring-do, rode the crest of the eighteenth century's political upheaval to a treasured spot in American lore. Many consider him the Father of the U.S. Navy.

Unfortunately, he died in Paris four years before the Bourbons succumbed and was buried there in St. Louis Cemetery. Fast forward more than a hundred years. Horace Porter, U.S. Ambassador to France under president Theodore Roosevelt (former Assistant Secretary to the Navy himself) paid to find Jones's mortal remains. Senior curator of the U.S. Naval Academy Museum Jim Cheevers said that after they pinpointed Jones's burial spot, his saviors had to knock through basement walls to

John Paul Jones finally came to rest at the
U.S. Naval Academy following a long odyssey.
COURTESY ANNAPOLIS AND ANNE ARUNDEL COUNTY CONFERENCE
AND VISITORS BUREAU

get to the casket. When opened, it revealed a remarkably intact cloth-
bound cadaver. The identifying criteria lined up, down to the 1780
bust of Jones by sculptor Jean Antoine Houdon. "Everything clicked,"
as Cheevers put it.

So, after a parade down the Champs-Élysées and boat ride on the
USS *Brooklyn*, the flagship of Roosevelt's naval squadron sent over
to pick him up, Jones arrived back to the States. His body arrived

in Annapolis in July 1905, while the modern-day Beaux Art campus was under construction. Jones lay in a special brick vault until 1906 when, at a big academy shindig, Theodore Roosevelt and dignitaries welcomed him home. And then—drumroll—the body was moved to Bancroft Hall, the academy's giant dormitory. There Jones stayed for another seven years in a spot that's right about where a student snack bar stands today. Plans for his crypt in the academy chapel ran aground over budget problems. What else is new? The experts figured out the finances, and Jones was moved into his new—and final—resting place on January 26, 1913.

The crypt and chapel are stops on the academy tour that prospective visitors can line up by calling (410) 293-8687 or going to www .usna.edu/visit.htm. Check the Web site for the latest security requirements for entry to the academy grounds.

Spring Fever
Annapolis

One year when the cold had lingered too long into March, a group of boat-y types over in the city's boat-y Eastport district took matters into their own hands. Gathering after work, they cracked open brewskis and tossed their socks into a burning pyre. Goodbye, winter! Hello, spring!

You must understand, "boat-y" is the operative word here. By March, these folks are past ready to get back on Chesapeake Bay. Part of their catechism includes living life sock-free. If you don't believe me, check the ankles of a boat-y type.

In recent years, this loose group has become formalized. Or as formal as Eastport gets. Folks now gather at the Annapolis Maritime Museum in Eastport (410-295-0104; www.annapolismaritimemuseum .org/calendar-socks.htm) at the vernal equinox for the annual Burning of the Socks. It's a public welcome to the warm-weather boating season. You don't need special skills—just take off your socks and toss them into the flames.

Jefferson Holland, poet laureate of Eastport (and, in a second role, the museum's director), can explain. Here's a portion of his *Ode to the Equinox*:

Them Eastport boys got an odd tradition.
When the sun swings to its Equinoxical position,
They build a little fire down along the docks,
They doff their shoes and they burn their winter socks.

Yes, they burn their socks at the Equinox;
You might think that's peculiar, but I think it's not,
See, they're the same socks they put on last fall,
And they never took 'em off to wash 'em, not at all . . .

Chesapeake boaters greet spring by burning their winter socks in Annapolis. COURTESY ANNAPOLIS MARITIME MUSEUM

★ ★

Taking the High Road

Annapolis

Question: Why would 20,000 people—most of them strangers to each other—go on a 4.5-mile hike together? Answer: Because they can. Who wouldn't want to spend a couple of hours ambling high above the glorious Chesapeake Bay?

Almost every year since 1975, the Bay Bridge Walk has taken place on an April day. Grab a hat and sunscreen, though. The sun gets fierce when it reflects off that much open water.

The William Preston Lane Jr. Memorial Bridge, better known as the Chesapeake Bay Bridge (www.baybridge.com), opened in 1952 after a years-long gestation period. At the time, it was the world's largest continuous overwater steel structure. A second span opened in 1973. Nowadays, more than twenty-five million vehicles cross the Bay Bridge every year—except for the day the Bay Bridge Walk takes place.

The walk has suffered a few blackout dates since it started: once due to a security alert and thrice due to rain. In 2008 and 2009 the walk cedes to construction. On the bright side, the Bay Bridge Preservation Project will be finished after that. Here's guessing it won't be a moment too soon for commuters and summer vacationers on their way to the ocean beaches.

The Governor Is In

Annapolis

Former Maryland governor Marvin Mandel eats Egg Beaters for breakfast. Yes, indeed, he does, with turkey bacon on the side. Born in 1920, the former chief executive must be watching his dietary p's and q's more closely than he did back in his legislator days when he favored corned beef and chopped liver sandwiches. But whatever he chooses from the menu, he can enjoy it in style.

He's got a lifetime reservation in the "Governor's Office," a special booth that's long been reserved for Maryland's governors past and

Three governors and one mayor join the Chick and Ruth's Delly crew and customers for the morning Pledge of Allegiance. COURTESY CHICK AND RUTH'S DELLY; PHOTOGRAPHER WEB WRIGHT

present at Chick and Ruth's Delly. Patrons recite the Pledge of Allegiance every morning at this Annapolis institution, where autographed photos of celebrities and politicians slather the yellow walls like a good schmear of cream cheese on your morning bagel. Sandwiches are named for politicians, who choose their namesake concoctions.

A red, white, and blue phone serves "the office." When vacant, the booth—the same orange as every booth in the long, narrow restaurant—is roped off. "If we know the governor's not coming in and we're jam-packed, judges or somebody special might use it," said Ted Levitt, the second-generation owner of the "delly" at 165 Main Street (410-269-6737; www.chickandruths.com).

★ ★

Ted's parents opened Chick and Ruth's in 1965, and Mandel, then Speaker of the Maryland House of Delegates, became a frequent customer. The "Governor's Office" opened when he was elevated to the state's highest office in 1967. Since then, Maryland's governors have reliably breakfasted at Chick and Ruth's the day after their inauguration. Former governor William Donald Schaefer (1987–1995) sometimes shares the booth with Mandel. Former governor Robert Ehrlich (2003–7) joined his predecessors and would sometimes show up mid-afternoon with his father and son for vanilla milk shakes. The governor who came in the least? "Probably Glendening," said Levitt, referring to Paris Glendening (1995–2003). Current governor Martin O'Malley comes in for breakfast, often with lieutenant governor Anthony Brown, said Levitt, who shared gubernatorial gustatory tales with me.

You wanna know what the Maryland politicos are up to? Now you know where to find out.

Trundling through Time
Annapolis

This may be the oldest modern-day story in the city's 300+-year-old book. A guy moves to Annapolis to be near his boat. He commutes to his job in the D.C. 'burbs, sails on the weekend, and fantasizes about cruising offshore when his magical retirement day arrives. Then it does. For D. L. Smith, though, sailing started to lose its luster. Here he was, retired, sailing and golfing—"wasting time," as he puts it—when he began to cast around for something else to do. An ad in the paper caught his eye: He could become a Colonial tour guide! And so he did. In the process he also became a student of the city's colorful history

The presence of three centuries of history in Annapolis cannot be overstated. Washington, Jefferson, their aides, and even the third president's doctor—all those patriots hung out during the city's Colonial "Golden Age." Mention Amos Garrett and you'd be surprised how many folks nod like they just saw him this morning down at City Dock. (Garrett was the city's first mayor, back in 1708.) Our protagonist, Mr.

The past meets the present when tourists take a Colonial tour aboard a Segway. COURTESY ANNAPOLIS AND ANNE ARUNDEL COUNTY CONFERENCE AND VISITORS BUREAU

Smith, donned a tricorn, learned how to wear a jabot, and, tourists in tow, took off to show them the city. Did you know that Annapolis has more eighteenth-century structures than any other city in the USA? Well, now you do.

"I've sort of fallen in love with that era," said Smith. "I have more clothes from the eighteenth century than the twenty-first."

★ ★

Much as he loves the past, Smith's a man of his own times. One day, he climbed on a Segway and whizzed off to inaugurate a new era in Colonial tourism. Scooting behind on Segways of their own came his touring clientele. Cops in NYC use Segways. Golfers in the UK use them. Why shouldn't tour guides in Colonial garb?

So if you see a guy clad in a blue wool cutaway and knee britches rolling through the city's brick sidewalks aboard a newfangled contraption, give him a holler at Capital City Colonials (410-295-9715; www .capitalcitycolonials.com). That's D. L. Smith, who has found a surefire way to steamroll the present into the city's ever-present past. After hours, he's also been known to run the Zamboni at the U.S. Naval Academy's ice rink. But that's another story . . .

Quoth the Raven I
Annapolis (Eastport)

In the back room of a clapboard house in the heart of Eastport, Howard Rogers opened a wooden drawer and extracted the tool he uses for carving. "This is the chisel I've had since I was sixteen and an apprentice," he said.

How many officially apprenticed British ship's joiners do you know? Even in Eastport, with its working maritime businesses (like sailmakers and an America's Cup designer), you're not likely to run across this kind of guy. Rogers, originally from Kent, England, worked on the River Medway until, at age twenty-six and itching for more creativity, he crossed the pond. He landed in Eastport thirty years ago.

Rogers works on, an old-schooler hand-carving 200 to 300 distinctive name boards per year for boats and yachts. Hanging in his gallery is a photograph of a 23-karat gold-leaf eagle that lives at Euro Disney (now Disneyland Paris) outside Paris. He carved that. Among the beautiful wooden pieces he's created is a tool trunk with a false bottom, a symphony of dovetailed joints. He works every day—early to bed and early to rise—with a break from 2:00 to 4:00 p.m. His paintings, mostly maritime, fill the spaces that wood and tools do not.

Howard Rogers, officially apprenticed ship's joiner, chisels away in Annapolis.

Come to 130 Severn Avenue and see this authentic bit of the old Annapolis boating scene. It's called the Raven Studio, a nod to the old sod, and a riff on the legend that the British Empire will fall when the ravens leave the Tower of London. They remain, incidentally, in the tower, even if Rogers left their country.

We Like It This Way

Annapolis (Eastport)

The Spa Creek Bridge separates Eastport, a maritime workingman's neighborhood, from the tonier Historic District. A decade ago when it was closed for repairs, Eastport's merchants and residents fretted because you couldn't get there from here—or vice versa. So what did they do? They seceded. As Brussels sprouts shot from military reenactors' muskets and horns blared from the Eastport Chamberpot Orchestra, passports (aka coupon books) were issued and a great movement was born.

These days, you'll spot "MRE" stickers on cars all along U.S. Highway 50 from Annapolis to Washington, D.C., and it seems to be an open secret around town that the Maritime Republic of Eastport (www.themre.org) boosted neighborhood property values. Now operating as a nonprofit, the republic gives donations from its annual events to local charities. You could probably join yourself, if you can figure out how and where its leaders meet.

"It was like searching for Brigadoon," said former MRE premier Mark Travaglini as he recounted his first attempt to attend a meeting. "I talked to one guy who was waiting for something to be happening, and he turned out to be a reporter looking for the same meeting. That happens a lot."

Ah well. The outfit's not supposed to be perfect, just "an enlightened democracy." Officers with titles like "Minister of Conscription" are elected annually, although "the joke is, if you don't come to the elections meeting, you might just end up with that office," said Travaglini.

Although Eastport's secession launched the republic, good old one-upmanship brought its everlasting security. Challenged to a tug-of-war across the Gulf of Eastport (aka Spa Creek—I guess they grabbed the water rights, too), downtown Annapolis denizens responded. "Truth be told, we don't check anybody's ID," said the premier. Word of mouth usually ensures two teams of thirty-three tuggers on each side of the gulf for three heats each November. Eastport usually wins.

If a tug-of-war is too competitive for your blood, consider the .05K race across the Spa Creek Bridge in spring (supposedly the shortest marathon on some official list) followed by Dog Day Afternoon, full of fun with canines. You'll probably meet some clever folks in the process.

Bump and Grind
Arcadia

Put on your thinking cap (or, in this case, perhaps a crash helmet) and imagine how you'd raise funds to pay for a volunteer fire department. A bake sale? Silent auction? Howzabout a fancy soiree?

None of the above, if you're the Arcadia Volunteer Fire Department. They turned to the people's motor sport. From spring until fall, they sponsor a popular demolition derby that draws folks from as far away as West Virginia. (For the schedule, see www.arcadiavfc.org.) Hey, at least they know how to find an EMT.

The ideal derby car should cost something under $100. Lucky drivers find a model from the 1970s, back when Detroit still made sedans huge and sturdy. Sledgehammers make quick work of windows and backseats. Driver's side doors are chained or welded shut, and painted a different color. The reason? No plowing into any driver's door. "That's the big no-no of the race," said Roslyn Snyder, the fire department's president.

I've never driven in a demolition derby, but something Ms. Snyder said made me wonder if it might not be more useful than, say, a spa day: "The rush is just unbelievable. It releases a lot. It's a good release for the year, to go out and bang up some cars."

Elizabeth Arden, watch your back.

★ ★

Davidsonville's famous mum mural blooms each fall at Doepkens Farm.

Painting with Posies

Davidsonville

The neighborhood phones start to ring as soon as Bill Doepkens plows the half-acre next to his barn. "What do you think it's going to be this year?" they ask. By June, when the first plantings go in, the formal guessing game begins. Everyone wants to solve their neighborhood's annual riddle.

Doepkens isn't telling. The subject of his annual planted mosaic of chrysanthemums, known locally as the "mum mural," shall be revealed in the fullness of time, aka fall. That's when mums bloom. "I like to surprise people," he said.

Over the growing season, the denizens of Davidsonville gaze up at Doepkens Farm, strategically located along busy Route 424 just north of even busier US 50, to puzzle over clues as they literally unfold and blossom.

★ ★

The tale of the Davidsonville mum mural began years ago, back before Doepkens changed his farm's primary crop from tobacco to flowers. "I saw a picture in the *Baltimore Sun* of this huge flower mural in England," he said. It was of van Gogh's *Sunflowers,* and required 250,000 bedding plants on ten acres. "And 250,000 sounds about right for ten acres," said the one man who should know. "Once I started growing mums, I thought it would be neat to try something on a smaller scale." So Doepkens did. In 1995 a sunset's rays spread across the barn's hill. Then came others that folks still talk about: the butterfly, and the hummingbird.

Back then, neighbor Brenda Jackson said, you could sometimes figure out the subject by looking at the mural's shape. "You had to wait until it was in almost full color to guess," she said. "Now, he's become so sophisticated, you really can't tell what it is until he puts the finishing touches to it."

A pair of wings constructed of bamboo poles and netting arranged in the barn's open doors proved to be the final clue in a recent mum mystery. That was after 2,600 plants of 92 varieties painted their picture. With that, a fire-breathing dragon burst out of the barn.

Land of Pleasant Picking
Deale

In a town best known for crab pickin', folks have taken up another form of "pickin'." They'll pick a guitar, a mandolin, or even a Dobro. On Friday nights they pick together, and then what you have is a bunch of folks just a'pickin' and a'grinnin'.

"Sometimes you can't get in the door," said Mark Sullivan, who bought the Good Deale Bluegrass Shop from a musician a few years back. I have driven past the place at 655 Deale Road for years and thought, "Jeez, what's that doing here?" Deale is Chesapeake waterman's territory, not Appalachian mountain man land. Watermen aren't bluegrass folks, are they? And then I got to thinking, the way the suburbs are gobbling up everything, by now Deale must be a satellite hub

Pickin' guitars, not crabs, at Good Deale
Bluegrass Shop along the Chesapeake Bay.

in the bluegrass constellation that revolves around Washington, D.C.
Talk to the guys who show up for the Friday jams, and more than one
will tell you he's from West Virginia, has been playing since the '50s,
and Washington is where the jobs were. Job-jobs as well as musician
jobs.

"Hillbilly music," said one guitar picker, that's what they called this
music before they called it "bluegrass." Once the group starts to sing-
ing, you hear that authentic high, lonesome voice. Settled on metal

folding chairs or a long church pew, two banjo players, one violin, two steel guitars, one mandolin, and six guitars jam across "Glendale Train," "Thought I Heard You Call My Name," and even a way cool version of "Lara's Theme," from the movie *Dr. Zhivago*. Among those assembled is a guy who once played with Patsy Cline, who lived west of Washington in Winchester, Virginia.

Seated behind the counter, Sullivan dispenses advice about guitar strings, mandolin bridges, and such. During the day, he oversees music lessons, repairs, and sales. You can reach him at (410) 867-2400.

Years back, somebody named the Chesapeake the "Land of Pleasant Living." The bluegrass folks have gone and co-opted that slogan. The back of the music store's T-shirt reads "Land of Pleasant Picking."

A Family Reunion
Ellicott City

Once upon a time, before six-lane highways and development, the three bears dwelled in their little concrete house, and it wasn't located in the pages of a fairy tale book. No, it stood in the Enchanted Forest on U.S. Highway 40 along with the Old Woman's Shoe, the Crooked Man and his Crooked House, Mother Goose, and even Willie the Whale—whomever, exactly, he may be in the annals of children's literature.

For years and years, starting in August 1955, little children came to see the three bears and their friends at the forest, which was a twenty-acre amusement park. But the little children grew older, and times changed. The Three Bears' House fell into disrepair. First came the cracks brought by rain, then vines and seedlings arrived, their tendrils sneaking through the cracks. Meantime, the nice people who owned the Enchanted Forest sold it. Today, the bears' friend, Old King Cole, sits atop a big sign where the forest once stood. It advertises the Enchanted Forest Shopping Center.

But two of the bears and many of their friends got lucky. With help from many, many others, a nice lady named Martha Clark, who grew

Enjoying Willy the Whale, once part of an amusement park, who now lives down on the farm near Ellicott City.

up near the Enchanted Forest, brought many of the Enchanted Forest figures to her farm, Clark's Elioak Farm, at 10500 Clarksville Pike (410-730-4049; www.clarklandfarm.com), which is open seasonally. They've also got a petting zoo. Now, children once again get to walk through the woods and see the big purple shoe where the old lady lives. Only now, they can buy their fall pumpkins next to Cinderella's coach.

Karma Mechanic
Ellicott City

Al was a well-known guy in allegedly specter-filled Ellicott City, a local auto mechanic who walked over to the bakery in his old mill town every morning for coffee. About fifteen years ago, he was working on a car when a heart attack struck. Al passed away.

Despite this sad turn of events, commerce moved forward. New owners bought his building and renovations commenced. Apparently, Al had mixed feelings about this. One day, from atop his ladder, one of the new owners looked down to find a man standing there. "Can I help you?" he asked. No one responded—and no one was there by the time he started down the rungs. This incident arose in conversation with a neighbor, who asked for the man's description. "Oh," said the neighbor. "It sounds like Al."

Maybe, maybe not. You know how these specter sightings go. But then, during one of the regular ghost tours run by the Howard County tourism office, the group stood in Al's former repair shop as the guide recounted Al's story. A basket fell off the wall, bounced about 5 feet across the room, and landed at the feet of one of the tour-goers. "She was visibly shaken," recounts tour organizer Ed Lilly. Her reaction wasn't just weird. Fellow tour-goers found themselves asking if she was OK, to which she responded: Al was working on her family car in his shop when he had the heart attack.

(Insert *Twilight Zone* theme here.)

Other alleged Ellicott City apparitions: Annie, the homesick student who died at the nineteenth-century women's school called the Patapsco Female Institute (now "stabilized" ruins in a historic park, although they must be spooky as heck after twilight), and the cooking ghost who supposedly sends mysterious aromas through the kitchen-free Ellicott City Court House.

Take Ye Haunted History of Olde Ellicott City tour at 8:30 p.m. Fridays and Saturdays from April through November. You can also catch a tour during the week if there's a full moon. For information, go to www.visithowardcounty.com/ghost_tours or call (410) 313-1900.

The Last One Standing

Ellicott City

Imagine how people felt as they watched the dawn of railroading, when the Iron Horse started running alongside the regular horses. It must have been like the first time you sent e-mail instead of a fax. Quantum steps, folks. Quantum steps.

In Ellicott City stands the nation's oldest surviving railroad station, an 1830–31 structure now affiliated with the Baltimore & Ohio Railroad Museum in Baltimore. That's fitting, because the Ellicott City station was the terminus for the B&O's first 13 miles of commercial track. The pretty stone museum is open from 11:00 a.m. to 4:00 p.m. Wednesday through Sunday and is located at 2711 Maryland Avenue. Call (410) 461-1945 or visit www.ecborail.com for details.

Insider Trading

Fort Meade

Mounted on the wall of the former Colony 7 Motel off the Baltimore-Washington Parkway is a replica of a very particular seal of these great United States. The original's in Washington, D.C., at the U.S. State Department, but its story belongs here, at the National Cryptologic Museum.

One 1946 day, when W. Averell Harriman was U.S. Ambassador to Russia, a group of Soviet schoolchildren assembled. While Cold War clouds gathered on the horizon, the little ones came in peace. To honor Harriman, the children presented him with the wooden U.S. seal. For six years, this symbol of goodwill between nations hung on the ambassador's office wall. Over time, our men in Moscow realized that what was said in the ambassador's office wasn't staying in the ambassador's office. Then Eisenhower-era spy Gary Powers was shot down flying his secret U2 over Russia. As both countries cried foul, U.S. Ambassador Henry Cabot Lodge presented the bugged U.S. seal to the United Nations.

Such are the curiosities residing in the museum near Fort Meade, which is easiest to reach if you get directions from its Web site, www.nsa.gov/museum. The phone number is (301) 688-5849.

When the Colony 7 folded, the super-secret National Security Agency (NSA) next door snapped the motel up. And through some kind of amazing diplomacy, the NSA, apparently known by wags as "No Such Agency," decided to turn it into a museum and display some of its code-breaking history. Germany's Enigma code-maker is here. Equipped with super-duper encryption powers of 3×10 to the 114th power (which means the machine had 17,576 options per letter of code that went out), Enigma looks like a typical old-fashioned machine with punch buttons. But this machine created a major threat to the Allies during World War II.

The Allies replied with a "bombe" that broke the German code. "Bombe" is a term that arrived via English translation. When the Poles made the first machine, they called it a "bomba." Seems the theory goes that while inventing the machine, mathematicians soothed their stress with an ice-cream dessert featuring a scoop of ice cream slathered in chocolate. Its name? A "bomba."

A Healthy Hobby
Freeland

Some people collect stamps. Others collect coins. Clyde Morris collects all kinds of old stuff. Irons. Feed bags. He's even got an antique cherry seeder and an antique peach peeler. When storage on his 500-plus-acre Baltimore County family farm overflowed, he was forced to act. He opened a museum, right next to his RV park.

"I've kind of always liked history, and I'm addicted to collecting junk," he cheerfully admitted as we prepared to tour the Morris Meadows Historic Preservation Museum, which is filled with stuff—but, boy, is it well organized and interesting.

The museum reflects life in the region during much of Morris's lifetime. As the fifth generation to live in the house where he was born,

★ ★

Morris remembers when blacksmith shops dotted the hilly landscape. So you may be interested in the odd machine—"a pile of gears," as he put it—which was used to make new wagon wheels. It's in the Blacksmith Shop, one of numerous booths, or "rooms," that depict a particular element of life. There's a one-room schoolhouse like the one Morris attended, with a dunce cap and a big bell that echoes through the museum. And since his wife, Virginia, loves music, there's a music room, with an old player piano and other instruments that Morris picked up at a Saturday-night auction 7 miles north in Pennsylvania, the source for many of his artifacts.

Clyde Morris collected so many artifacts from old-style country living that he opened his own museum in Freeland.

Some things predate Morris, but he just couldn't resist the buy. My favorite is the meat cutter used by Union troops at nearby Gettysburg. A series of blades chopped meat on a cutting board that's a cleaved log. And who knew butter churns came in so many varieties? Then there's the 1877 Geiser threshing machine, just like the one Morris and his father used to thresh wheat.

There's much more, including salutes to local veterans from this World War II U.S. Navy veteran. To see Morris's museum, give him a call at (410) 329-6636 or check his website at http://www.morris meadows.us/.

Quoth the Raven II
Glen Arm

A century ago, the gabled Gothic-style Ravenshurst Mansion proudly stood atop a hill in the Dulaney Valley overlooking an expansive landscape, secure in its roots reaching back to the early 1800s. Grandees arrived, including Confederate president Jefferson Davis, who, according to news reports from the old *Baltimore News American,* convalesced from his two-year, postwar prison sentence at the manse. The thirty-six-room house rambled across two and a half floors, and was topped by a domed cupola and octagonal tower.

Land rich and cash poor as time went by, Ravenshurst's owners started selling off pieces of the property. And we're not talking about an acre or three. Times were tough and assets were evident: Hand-finished wood floors and wood trim from rooms were sold to dealers. By the time the last of the heirs died as the twentieth century wore on, the place looked like a horror movie set. It needed new owners—or something. But there was a catch: A tenant retained lifetime residency rights.

Vandals ruled, but historic-preservation types were interested in saving the house. They stepped over gaping holes in the flooring as they picked their way around, according to one of my sources who was there.

Meantime, fine homes sprung up around the mansion. Even after Ravenshurst was sold in the early 1980s for $15,000, the new owner had nothing but trouble on his hands. He was stuck, according to an article from the old *News American*. He couldn't restore the house, and the lingering lifetime tenant hardly helped matters.

Finally, fate intervened. Fire broke out one Christmas Eve. The former grande dame, now just a spooky old house, burned to the ground.

The End.

Hot Diggity

Glen Burnie

Step inside Ann's Dari-Crème and wow! You're instantly in line! Not only is the place a) tiny, but b) it's always packed. Expect little elbow room at one of eight stools, the front-row seats for the cashier-and-kitchen show on the other side of the counter. Ann's combines prompt service with showmanship that involves daring feats of memory. It's the ultimate paperless transaction. To wit:

"Your double, your single, your shake, and your fry, $13.64," remembers the cashier, formally known as a "taker" because she takes the orders. "Whole cheesesteak, your fry, your drink, $8.94," she tells another customer. One man reads a long order of six sandwiches, four french fries, two Cokes, and two milk shakes, and the taker only has to double-check one item. Even then, she has everything right but the onions on one cheeseburger. Want those fried?

Since 1951 milk shakes and subs have issued from the grill, but Ann's star menu item is the specialty hot dogs. A foot long and two to the roll, they're cooked in constant procession. One recent fall Friday, 767 folks came in the door and 467 hotdogs went out. You can smell french fries from the parking lot.

At Ann's, "they're fast, and they remember everything," confides a mother waiting in line. Manager Pat Schreiber, who's worked here since the month after her 1965 high school graduation, knows that

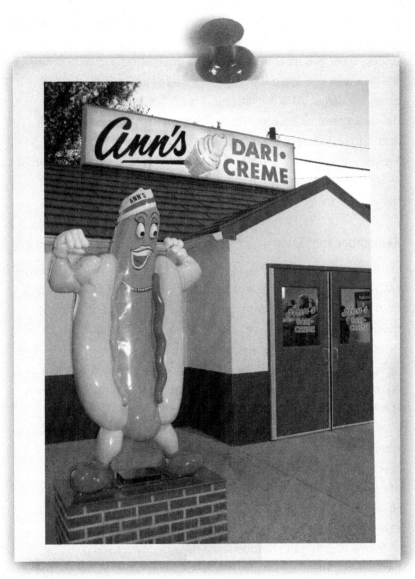

Hot diggity! Get your foot-long at Ann's
Dari-Crème in Glen Burnie.

★ ★

she and her "girls" are a huge part of Ann's draw: "A lot of people tell me they're here to watch the show."

Boys meet girls at Ann's Dari-Crème. Business associates look for the landmark hot dog out front, which makes this an easy place to meet. Located at 7918 Ritchie Highway (410-761-1231; www.anns daricreme.com), right alongside the entrance to Marley Station Mall, Ann's occupies a spot where we've come to expect a franchise. As the story goes, back when the mall was developed (it opened in the 1980s), Ann's owners opted not to move out of its way. And thank heavens for that.

Remember the Graw
Havre de Grace

Maryland's got serious horse-racing bona fides. Early thoroughbreds from Belair Mansion in Bowie, for instance, had a lot to do with the development of the American thoroughbred. And you've no doubt heard of Baltimore's Preakness Stakes.

But have you heard of "The Graw"? I'm thinking no. It sounds like an undesirable that grows in gardens or garbage cans after hot, heavy humidity. Or something that gets stuck in your throat.

Au contraire! The Graw was a famous Havre de Grace racetrack where legends like Man O' War, Sea Biscuit, and War Admiral raced. It opened in 1913 and closed in 1950. Its clubhouse, now owned by the Maryland National Guard, still stands. And it was formally called the Havre de Grace Racetrack. So, I just had to ask, why on earth was it called "The Graw"?

Seems that that this Susquehanna riverside town's French name, bestowed by Marquis de Lafayette, got Americanized. In French, the word for "grace"—grâce—is pronounced "graw." What better name for the local track?

In mid-October, a new festival called Celebrate the Graw tips its hat to those colorful racing days of yore, about which you can learn more at www.mainstreethdg.com.

You're never too old to collect Star Wars toys, as evidenced by the Star Toys Museum in Linthicum. SARA MORELL

The Force

Linthicum

When in the course of human events it becomes necessary for one man to convince his buddies to join the Toys R Us drawing for a giant Millennium Falcon—and he wins—the force is clearly with him.

That's what happened to Thomas Atkinson, whose Star Toys Museum is open by appointment at his house at 811 Camp Meade Road (410-859-1261; www.startoysmuseum.org).

Collector Atkinson saw the first *Star Wars* movie when it came out in 1977, the year he turned thirteen. By the end of that ground-breaking annum, he possessed a couple of *Star Wars* T-shirts, the movie's vinyl soundtrack, and a poster or two. He'd only just begun. When twelve little action-figure characters came out in '78, Atkinson followed his comic-book-collecting older brother's advice: Buy two and only open one.

Since then, he's amassed a collection that currently lists approximately 12,000 items in his database. Who wouldn't open a museum? Visitors who check out the Star Toys Museum will see those original boxed dozen figures. The Millennium Falcon, Hans Solo's spaceship, is 6 feet long and was originally a store display. It hovers over much of the collection—which, by the way, is not all on display at once. It does, however, include Atkinson's first light saber, which doesn't work anymore. And a TIE Bomber, still in the box.

What *is* the *Star Wars* draw?

"It was the combination of everything," said Atkinson. "The visuals. The way the characters inhabited the *Star Wars* galaxy. Here was Luke Skywalker, and he was living in a world where there were aliens and robots and spaceships and magic and so much amazing stuff and he's completely bored with it.

"All he wants to do is get away from where he is and have adventures."

Sounds like he needs to visit the Star Toys Museum.

A Natural Fact
Linthicum

The William P. Didusch Center for Urologic History is located in the shiny corporate-looking American Urological Association headquarters. Well, that makes good sense. Who else is going to celebrate this vital function?

The museum, located at 1000 Corporate Boulevard (410-689-3785; www.urologichistory.museum) near Baltimore-Washington International Airport, was founded to preserve the extensive collection of medical illustrations by William P. Didusch, who also was the museum's first curator. Didusch worked for years at the Johns Hopkins Brady Urological Institute. (This is a major-league operation that, incidentally, was initially funded by and named for patient "Diamond" Jim Brady, a Gilded Age dandy and businessman.) Visitors can check out the museum during weekdays from 9:00 a.m. to 5:00 p.m. and catch a tour by appointment.

Visitors learn that the cystoscope—designed for peering inside—evolved ever so slowly from a contraption illuminated via a candle to fiberoptics. The extensive display of scopes over the years is proof that there's no reason to reinvent the wheel; when you see the scopes, you'll see what I mean.

There's some weird stuff here, like the simple tool stashed inside walking sticks or umbrellas. It's a catheter, once used by gentlemen of a certain age who needed to easily manage the daily discomforts wrought by an enlarged prostate. Practical, no?

Annual exhibits have ranged over urology's fertile and necessary terrain, from medical quackery to the recently displayed "Plagues and Pestilence." From the looks of it, folks have thought of everything.

Rage On
Lutherville

You've heard about the great Chicago fire, when Old Lady Leary's cow—so they say—kicked the lantern over. That was 1871. Then there was the 1906 earthquake that clobbered San Francisco. You've probably heard about that one, too. What you may not know is that Baltimore nearly burned to cinders in 1904. Crews from as far away as New York came to help fight the two-day blaze that took out the most important square mile of business in the city.

It started on a quiet Sunday morning, February 7, most likely when a lit match or cigar wasn't properly extinguished. The alarm went off at John Hurst & Co., between Hopkins Place and Liberty Street by what was then called German Street (now Redwood Street). Around noon, the building exploded and the blaze took off. Flames leapt across the rooftops and burned down to the streets. A stiff winter wind changed direction four times during the conflagration and complicated efforts to contain the blaze. On top of that, different fire company hoses had differently sized couplings, so a lot of hoses couldn't screw into Baltimore's hydrants (which later led to standardization). About noon on Monday, the firefighters made a last stand along the Jones Falls. Thirty-

★ ★

seven steam fire engines pulled water from the falls, and stopped the blaze.

Among the disaster's heroes was a mighty white horse named Goliath. Tethered to a 65-foot water tower at the Hurst building, he wheeled around and pulled the tower to safety moments before the building blew. For the rest of his nineteen-year firefighting career, he wore scars on his flank. The water tower, later updated with a motorized cab, is on display at the Fire Museum of Maryland at 1301 York Road (410-321-7500; www.firemuseummd.org). It's one of several pieces of equipment from the Great Fire in an extensive collection documenting fire equipment through the years. Don't miss it.

The museum is open on Saturdays from 10:00 a.m. to 4:00 p.m. May through December, and Wednesday through Saturday from 10:00 a.m. to 4:00 p.m. and Sunday from 1:00 to 4:00 p.m. June through August.

Yew Ought to See This
Monkton

The late Harvey S. Ladew's topiary gardens are like his pal Cole Porter's lyrics. What we have here is "one of those fabulous flights." Well, make that numerous fabulous flights. Pull into the front drive of Ladew Topiary Gardens, his former estate, and you'll see what I mean. Leaping over the hedge to your left, a fellow rider right behind, is a foxhunter on horseback. His hounds lead. Across the drive? But of course: the fox. All are frozen in action via the magic of topiary, the art of shrub sculpting.

And they're just the first of the many surprises at the house and gardens at 3535 Jarrettsville Pike (410-557-9466; www.ladewgardens .com; open seasonally).

A wealthy denizen of the Jazz Age, Ladew trotted the globe and brought home what he liked. The idea for stylish British gardens certainly was one. He moved to Maryland's hunt country from Long Island in 1929 and soon blessed his estate with his whims. His Colonial

Deluxe shrub sculptures grow in whimsical fashion in Maryland hunt country.

house, for instance, doesn't just have an oval-shaped library, it has an oval-shaped library with a false door—or is it a little hidden room?—that leads to the patio. Outside, hundreds of topiaries fill twenty-two acres of garden rooms.

Twelve swans float atop "waves" of yew and form the back border to "The Great Bowl," a gently sloping lawn centered by a reflecting pool. In the Topiary Sculpture Garden, seahorses rise from their shrubs, as does a V-for-Victory sign. It's trimmed into a bush located across from Winston Churchill's hat. After all, Ladew was a Churchill-era kinda guy. Perhaps that particular inspiration came from another of his social set, the former King Edward VIII (the Duke of Windsor to us serfs), who once borrowed Ladew's horse for a hunt.

A Rocky Ripple

Owings Mills

It took six years for Baltimore Colts legend Johnny Unitas to land in the Pro Football Hall of Fame. Ditto Cal Ripken Jr. He retired from the Baltimore Orioles in 2001 and was a National Baseball Hall of Famer by 2007.

Then there's Isaac Tyson Jr., 1996 inductee into the National Mining Hall of Fame and Museum in far-off Leadville, Colorado. The Maryland mining pioneer waited 135 whole years for recognition from an industry few would link to the Free State. Tyson pioneered the American chromium industry from what's now suburban Baltimore. In the process, he may have inspired the yellow cabs we hail today.

The son of wealthy Quakers, Tyson established chromium mines, including one at what's now Soldier's Delight Natural Environment Area (410-461-5005; www.dnr.state.md.us/publiclands/central/soldiers.html), 1,900 acres with 7 miles of trails. Tyson knew that chromite occurs in serpentine rock, which runs through the property. This is a type of metamorphic rock that surfaced 500 million years ago when the continental shelves collided and shoved heated, pressurized rock from deep in the earth up to the crust. The rock now snakes like a dotted line from Georgia north to Quebec's Gaspe Peninsula, then across the Atlantic to the Shetland Islands, explained mining engineer Johnny Johnsson. He runs a twice-annual mining-history hike at Soldier's Delight to tell about the rock, and show folks the state's best-preserved metal-mine entrance.

Back in his day, Tyson developed and monopolized the chromium industry. He shipped the stuff to Europe in big barrels. There, it was used to produce the popular new paint color of—you guessed it—chromium yellow. When England's trendsetting Princess Charlotte painted her carriage bright yellow, Tyson must have heard ringing cash registers from across the Atlantic. The masses followed suit, leaving in their wake a tradition so strong that yellow remains a popular color for cabs today.

A Hard Place

Port Deposit

Tiny Port Deposit is wedged between the wide Susquehanna River and rock-filled cliffs. While it's hard to take your eyes off the former, you can't miss the latter. Note the rock outcroppings. This is the famous Port Deposit granite, quarried here until 1970.

Major buildings made from Port Deposit granite include the U.S. Treasury Building in Washington, D.C., and the New Jersey side of the Lincoln Tunnel. In Maryland, you'll find it embedded in Baltimore's Fort McHenry.

Port Deposit is proud of its homegrown stone.

The stone's hometown bears its stamp. Every church here—five in all—is built of the stuff. It's also evident in fanciful remnants of the largesse left behind by Jacob Tome, a local self-made baron. My favorite of Tome's landmarks is called the Steps to Liberty, which climb up the town-side cliff. Local historian Erika Quesenberry, who shared much about her beloved "Port" with me, provided the lowdown:

Built about 1903, the steps replaced an earlier, steep staircase ("Jacob's Ladder") built during construction of the Tome School for Boys. Alas, they were removed because the boys instead used them as a playground. The new Steps to Liberty allowed access to the school and, later, to the now-closed Bainbridge Naval Training Center, which opened in 1942. It's said that young sailors on R & R coined the name.

Bridge to the Past
Relay

In 1835 the powers that be opened the Thomas Viaduct spanning the Patapsco River between Relay and Elkridge. This spectacular feat of engineering was the nation's first multispan railroad bridge. Benjamin H. Latrobe Jr., scion of the architecture and engineering legend, designed the viaduct, built at the tiny spot called Relay, just west of Elkridge.

The Baltimore & Ohio Railroad put Relay on the map as a terminal for trains back when they were still drawn by horses. To this day, trains rumble over the viaduct. What's not around any more are the mill towns that once thrived upriver, long ago swept away by floods. Downriver, the major Colonial port of Eldridge Landing silted in. If you visit the town of Elkridge, turn west at Levering Avenue and, trust me, you'll see the viaduct soon enough.

To find out more about the viaduct and the area, now Patapsco Valley State Park, go to www.dnr.state.md.us/publiclands/central /patapscovalley.html.

John Waters muse Divine rests in peace north of Baltimore.

Divine's Grave

Towson

Way back when early postwar baby boomers could shock their parents, budding movie director John Waters launched his chum Harris Glenn Milstead toward stardom. In his tight-fitting dresses and painted boomerang eyebrows, outsize Milstead was, in a famous word, "Divine."

Divine danced through *Polyester,* famous for "Odorama," with its audience participation via scratch-and-sniff cards. Yes, you knew which smell to skip—especially if you'd heard about *Pink Flamingos,* in which Divine did worse than simply smell the, uh, prop at hand. He created the role of Edna Turnblad in *Hairspray* back when John Travolta was making *Look Who's Talking.*

Sadly, Divine died at age forty-two of excess weight and sleep apnea, according to IMDb.com. Today, he rests in view of the Towson Town Center Macy's in a small hillside cemetery called Prospect Hill. Lipstick kisses dot the grave, and graffiti turns up all the time.

★ ★

"Thanks" and "The Mother of America" were scrawled across the marble the day I visited. The headstone was topped with one small black mule. Its rhinestones sparkled like Divine.

Way Down Yonder in the Pumpkin Patch
Westminster

Standing in the front yard of the house where he grew up, John Chambers points to one of the most famous footnotes in U.S. history. Where spruce trees now grow, stray volunteer pumpkins spent one—emphasis on the *one*—fabled growing season.

You see, John's father was Whittaker Chambers, a former Communist who became a leading figure in a Cold War–era drama. Long story short, Chambers went to FDR's administration with information in the late 1930s, worried about Communist influence on U.S. policy, according to his son. Years passed. Chambers was writing for *Time* magazine when, in 1948, the House Committee on Un-American Activities got hold of Chambers's then-forgotten story. A young Richard Nixon rode the tale to his own political prominence, and a State Department higher-up named Alger Hiss ended up convicted of perjury.

John was in junior high and high school in Westminster when all of this went on, a kid who'd come home to find reporters camped on his lawn. As for the pumpkin patch? One night, the senior Chambers needed a place—fast—to hide some evidence. So he whittled out a pumpkin in the patch, stuck the documents in, and placed the pumpkin back in its spot. John told me that the plot was really the family strawberry patch but he'd lost some pumpkin seeds while moving compost when doing his chores.

Today, visitors sometime wander into this National Historic Landmark 30 miles west of Baltimore, where John lives. He points to the outbuilding at 632 East Sawmill Road, where one of these days he plans to install his father's papers so folks can review them if they'd like. He's a son who watched his parents struggle, and believes that sharing their story shows people that life goes on, for better or worse.

4

Southern Maryland

Here's the thing about Southern Maryland. You've got to define it properly. Old-timers insist that southern Anne Arundel County and southern Prince George's County join Charles, Calvert, and Saint Mary's Counties to make up Southern Maryland. This used to be tobacco-farming country.

More modern wags—myself among them—are giving way to modern definitions. For purposes of this book, I've included Beltway-side Prince George's County in the Suburban Washington, D.C., chapter and all of Anne Arundel in the Central Maryland chapter. Nice and neat, see?

Turns out those old rural ties are hard to pull apart. Forgive my geographical transgression when I revert to the old ways. One of Southern Maryland's distinct curiosities—although hardly a funny one—is the role it played in John Wilkes Booth's escape after he shot president Abraham Lincoln. It's a straight shot from Washington, D.C., across the Potomac River into Virginia via the old definition of Southern Maryland.

Southern Marylanders have found ways to celebrate the prehistoric sharks who swam here when this land was covered by water. They turn out by the thousands to toast spring with a mai tai. A former state senator shows up in his beat-up sneakers every year to orchestrate an annual "wade-in" to see how clear the Patuxent River's looking and welcome summer.

At a church in Port Republic, jousters—yes, jousters—spear their quarry, a small ring, at a tournament held every single summer. And I mean every summer, for more than 140 years. After all, jousting is the Maryland state sport.

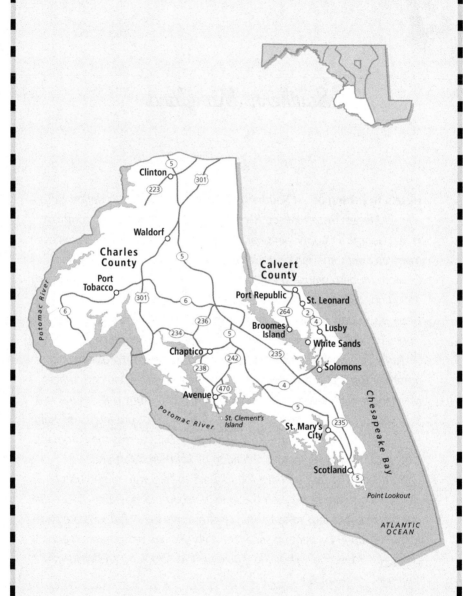

Southern Maryland

A folksy former senator tests the clarity of the Patuxent River the old-fashioned way.

Wading in the Water

Broomes Island

Every second Sunday in June since 1988, Bernie Fowler dons the same pair of white sneakers (now with holes in the big toe), and heads for the Patuxent River to wade in the water.

No, a white-robed gospel choir doesn't rise up behind him. But he's hardly alone. Over the years, hundreds have clasped hands and entered the river for the Bernie Fowler Wade-In. They stop when the former senator, a six-footer, can't see his feet. The summer ritual is repeated not for religious reasons, but to check the river's clarity. It's so simple, you wish every bureaucrat in America would c'mon down and see how it's done.

The depth from the waterline on his denim overalls (he wears those every year, too) to Fowler's feet is measured and graphed onto the

annual "sneaker index." In 2008 it was 28 inches. The river's been worse, but it's still not as clear as it was during the World War II veteran's youth. Back then, Fowler could wade practically shoulder-deep and still see grass and crabs in the Patuxent, a Chesapeake Bay tributary and subject of massive bay cleanup efforts.

The Patuxent wade-in has spawned a whole bunch of Maryland wade-ins, often featuring Fowler. That must make him the granddaddy of the wade-in. Since his serious message has a political angle, it's no surprise that the politicos show up at Broomes Island. Take Maryland congressman Steny Hoyer, House Majority leader, recently spotted in thigh-high water next to his pal Fowler. His sneakers didn't look so new either.

The annual gathering takes place in the early afternoon. On the second Sunday in June, drive to Broomes Island in Calvert County and keep going straight. You can't miss it.

Left Behind

Calvert County

Did you know the Atlantic Ocean receded eight million years ago? Me either, until a scientist told me. The sediments that make up the Calvert Cliffs were left with fossils of whales, dolphins, and plenty of shark teeth—as the locals well know.

Turns out a remnant of what those sharks may have been trying to eat with those teeth has been left behind as well. It's called a coprolite. That's scientific for "fossilized feces." The teeth whose marks remain in this rare specimen may have been rummaging around for dinner, or they may have bitten into the intestines of what turned out to be lunch. Amazing that such a thing still exists, isn't it? Three coprolites bearing intricate fossilized feathers also have been found, birds probably dined on by a prehistoric crocodile.

The coprolites aren't on display yet, but plenty of fossils from the cliffs (where digging is banned unless you have specific permission from the landowners) can be seen at the Calvert Marine Museum, which is located on Highway 2/4 right where you enter Solomons Island. You really can't miss it, but you can call (410) 326-2042 or check www.calvertmarinemuseum.com if you think you might.

Queen of Tobacco Road
Charles County

How's this for a Maryland beauty queen title: Miss Crustacean. She hails from the Eastern Shore crabbing town of Crisfield. I thought nothing could beat it. Then I ran across Queen Nicotina, who rules over the Charles County Fair each fall.

Queen Nicotina XVII herself told me in a phone interview that the name comes from the word *nicotinum,* the botanical name for the flowers that blossom on the tobacco plant. For eons Charles County was the epicenter of tobacco country. The locals crowned their fair's first queen in 1931, and unlike the plant for which she is named, Queen Nicotina continues to reign on. She's only missed one year, and that was during World War II.

Come visit the fair in mid-September and see for yourself. You can learn all about it at www.charlescountyfair.com.

A Carbine and Field Glasses
Clinton

Clinton is located in Prince George's County, officially part of the Sub-urban Washington, D.C. chapter. However, many have long viewed the county's southernmost region as part of Southern Maryland. Since the Surratt House is not far from Dr. Samuel Mudd's house (see "The Hatbox Splint" later in this chapter), and both sites figure prominently in the story of president Abraham Lincoln's assassination, let's make an exception to the rule.

The Surratt House was a tavern, hotel, polling place, and post office located on the stagecoach route to Washington, D.C. It was built in 1852 by John Surratt, who died two years before his family and tavern

★ ★

became embroiled in the 1865 Lincoln assassination plot. Inside the Surratt House and Tavern at 9118 Brandywine Road, guides in period garb tell about the family Surratt. The house is generally open Thursday through Sunday from 11:00 a.m. to 3:00 p.m., and closed from mid-December to mid-January.

Mary Surratt, known to history as the first woman ever hanged by the U.S. government, moved to Washington in the fall of 1864 and opened a boardinghouse. Left running the tavern was a Southern sympathizer. Both of Mary's sons favored the South, one as a soldier and one as a spy. The spy, John Jr., apparently was involved in John Wilkes Booth's original kidnapping plot, which failed and became an assassination plan. Booth is known to have visited the Washington boardinghouse, as well as to have stopped at the tavern as he escaped from Ford's Theatre. As always, check the history books for details, because there are plenty.

At the Surratt House today, you can see Mary's writing desk and center parlor table. You'll also see a 1863 Spencer repeating carbine, the same model as the one hidden in the house as part of the kidnapping scheme. The day of Lincoln's assassination, Mary (still running the Washington boardinghouse) is said to have told her tenant at the tavern that the "shooting irons would be called for that night." Booth spent five minutes on a horse outside the tavern a few hours after he shot the president, while a friend ran in and fetched a gun. Seems Mary also found a way to slip him some field glasses.

Tales of unexplained footsteps and other such ghostly events have been told about the house, which, like the Dr. Mudd House, is part of a twice-annual Booth Escape Route tour that sells out fast. For info, check the Surratt House Web site, www.surratt.org, or call (301) 868-1121.

Happy Birthday, Dear Charles County . . .

In 1958 a giant three-tiered cake sprouted from the median of U.S. Highway 301, the major north–south highway through the state. The state won't let you build cakes (or anything) in public median strips anymore, as the organizer of Charles County's 350th birthday learned in 2008, but that didn't stop celebration organizer Bobbie Baldus from reaching back into the mists of time.

After asking around to find out what folks recalled from '58, Baldus learned that memories of that big ole cake remained sharp. So, she rounded up volunteers to make not just one cake, but five, so the county's five regions could all celebrate. Built from plans replicating the '58 cake, each 24-foot confection was a little bit different. One had pink trim, and one had yellow. "Frosting" might be stucco. Candles made from 5-foot PVC pipe candles lit the top of each cake.

As I write this, there is a cake along US 301. Only this time, it sits on private property.

A traditional, if outsized, symbol celebrated Charles County's 350th birthday.

SARA MORELL

The handprints of its iconic late owner stand at Vera's, still operating in Lusby. SARA MORELL

Following in Her Gold Lamé Footsteps

Lusby

It ain't the Hollywood Walk of Fame, but for Vera Freeman, it's perfect. The late diva ruled her tiki-inspired empire for decades, and pressed her hands into the cement at her beloved Vera's White Sands Beach Club & Restaurant not too long before she died.

So, the hostess who arrived fifty years ago in rural Calvert County with her husband—he was "optometrist to the stars" in Hollywood—will never really leave.

Her hand-picked successors, Steve Stanley and Lisa Marie DelRicco, renovated the restaurant-club at 1200 White Sands Drive (410-586-1182; www.verasbeachclub.com), which Vera and Doc Freeman carved out of the scenic St. Leonard Creek countryside. Sure, some changes have taken place. For instance, diners can now pick crabs and the piano man's been replaced by bands. But don't worry. "I think it will always have that Vera twist," said Stanley.

To that end, the grand portrait of Vera that used to hang over the bar oversees the new entryway. There she is, wearing a Balinese-looking headdress. A large metal diving helmet, one of Vera's many collectibles from her world travels, is also displayed. And, yes, that is a suit of armor.

"Yes, we rebuilt," said Stanley. "But the soul of it came from her and her husband years ago—when it was nothing but woods."

I didn't check, but I'm guessing the bartender still mixes drinks with pink umbrellas, too.

Charge, Fair Knight

Port Republic

Let's play a word association game. I say jousting. You say . . . what? Sir Galahad? Sir Lancelot? Anybody can see why those names leap to mind. Here in the Free State, however, the correct answer is: Maryland state sport.

The traditions of Sirs Galahad and Lancelot are not forgotten by its Maryland practitioners, despite jousting's traditional past as a farm custom called "tournament." "Charge, fair maid" (or "charge, fair knight") really is what the announcer says when Maryland's official state sportspeople begin their individual rounds of competition. These might include kids from the Giddy-Up 4H Horse and Pony Club, or multiple generations of jousters from a single family.

★ ★

For more than 140 years, Christ Church has been the site of a jousting tournament. Jousting is Maryland's official state sport. JOSHUA GILLELAN

On the last Saturday in August, a traditional favorite in the Maryland jousting schedule takes place. And I do mean traditional. That's the Calvert County Jousting Tournament, hosted at Christ Church in Port Republic. In 2008 the 142nd tournament took place. (And the church parish is no youngster either. It dates to 1672.)

"The rings are hung. The track is clear. Charge, fair knight," comes the call. On a hot, humid day, the horse kicks up dust as its rider, sturdy in his stirrups, aims his lance at a small ring hanging under a squared arch. Will he spear it? He gets three tries.

The sport has its quirks: You can't buy a lance in a store, so beginners have been known to start out with broomsticks before finding their way to the lance-making community. The knights and ladies think up their own names, like "Knight of Little Woods." And the rings come in different sizes, the smallest being the size of a Life Saver piece of candy.

Jousting arrived with Maryland's early settlers, who amused themselves with tournaments. Well into the twentieth century, tournaments were major social events. In 1962 jousting became the official state sport. If you can't make the Christ Church tournament, check the Maryland Jousting Tournament Association schedule for other options: www.geocities.com/marylandjousting. It's well worth your time, fair maids and knights.

Legend of the Blue Dog
Port Tobacco

Port Tobacco's European settlers arrived about 1634, so, as you might guess, the town's history comes with a juicy ghost story. This one's so good, it's been floating around for at least a century.

Seems that one night after the Revolutionary War, a greedy fellow named Henry Hanos killed Charles Thomas Sims and his dog when Sims was heading home from a tavern. Hanos stole some gold and Sims's deed to an estate, which he buried on Rose Hill Road outside town.

The thief returned to the scene of the crime, but whatever steps he took to cover his tracks couldn't outwit Sims's avenger. That's right: When Henry tried to dig up the booty, the ghost of Charles Sims's dog chased him off. It is said that it was a blue dog. Soon after, Henry took sick and died.

Boo!
Scotland

The first time Kim Hammond went to Point Lookout Lighthouse at night, she was there for one reason and one reason alone: She wanted to experience a ghost. Like zillions of others (or so it seems), she wasn't disappointed. "We were all sitting downstairs, quiet, observing. Phantom footsteps walked right up to me when nobody was there," she said.

I don't know how you measure what structure is more haunted than another, but there's little question that this particular lighthouse has a strongly spooky reputation. Located on a peninsula where the Potomac River dumps into Chesapeake Bay, the circa 1830 structure has overseen the Union's prisoner-of-war camp at Point Lookout, as well as a hospital built especially for smallpox victims. Life in a nineteenth-century lighthouse was no picnic, what with the isolation, heat, and limited freshwater supply.

So who's at the light? "There's a lot of speculation," said Hammond. Perhaps a former lighthouse keeper. Or maybe someone associated with the Civil War, like the lighthouse keeper's daughter who supposedly claimed she hid soldiers in the basement. One group of paranormal investigators recorded a sailor from a sunken ship identifying himself by name. Allegedly.

Hammond, a paranormal expert, told me she thinks the lighthouse is active because it's not overly visited. And she also has a theory about why ghosts may exist: "The love of a place or a tragic ending can cause people to stay."

The light is part of Point Lookout State Park at 11175 Point Lookout Road (301-872-5688; www.dnr.state.md.us/publiclands/southern/pointlookout.html). It's open on the first Saturday of every month. In addition, paranormal nights are held by a group trying to restore the light. For information, visit www.pointlookoutlighthouse.com.

Artistry is found in all places at Annmarie Garden in Solomons. SARA MORELL

Rooms of One's Own

Solomons

Annmarie Garden sounds like a place full of wisteria and fine china, but that's hardly the case. This is a serious sculpture garden and arts center, located at 13480 Dowell Road (410-326-4640; www.annmarie garden.org) and related to Washington, D.C.'s modern Hirshhorn Museum. But that doesn't mean this place is all solemnity.

Enter the whimsical ceramic gates, which look like they're topped by white waves. Glimpse Calvert County's history in the bronze oyster tonger or take the Stonehenge approach and contemplate life in the

stone sculpture called *Council Ring.* Then duck into the contemporary building to see what's hanging. (The building's 2008 opening exhibit included works by Pablo Picasso and Joan Miró.)

Before you leave, do visit the loo. No kidding. Named "Best Restroom" by a local newspaper, these are works of mosaic art that HGTV should study. They were birthed by the mother of invention. During the garden's construction, volunteers gathered a ton of mismatched tile and got busy. Check out the cool tree in one of the women's room stalls. Colored tile pinwheels encircle replicas of the front gates on another wall.

That's worth a "Best of" vote, don't you think?

Sharkfest!
Solomons

Move over, Jaws. Way back when, a super-duper great white shark lived around Solomons Island. He was formally known as *Carcharodon megalodon,* grew up to 52 feet, and swam in the prehistoric Miocene Sea that covered this part of Maryland clear over to Washington, D.C.

It's been seven million years since he lived in Chesapeake Bay, but that doesn't stop folks from reminiscing. Megalodon lives on at the Calvert Marine Museum at 14150 Solomons Island Road (410-326-2142; www.calvertmarinemuseum.com), or at least his 38-foot skeletal replica does. He's a great excuse to celebrate Sharkfest! on the second Saturday in July. Another excuse comes in the form of sharks' teeth, a well-known find on nearby bayside beaches that you can see at the museum. Did you know that sharks' teeth operate kinda like a conveyor belt? There are three rows on top and three on the bottom. When one falls out, another comes right on in.

Sharkfest! kicks the shark festivities up a notch, especially because real sharks arrive courtesy of a local enthusiast. Come check out those pearly whites.

Shark! Learn more about these creatures who once swam here at the Calvert Marine Museum in Solomons.
COURTESY CALVERT MARINE MUSEUM

Tai One On

Solomons

Not too long ago, 22,000 people showed up over a weekend in little Solomons to celebrate the definitive arrival of spring. No, it wasn't the robins building nests. Daffodils sprouting? Fuggedabout it.

The masses rejoiced because the Tiki Bar reopened, where the secret-recipe mai tai is the order of the day. This has been going on for

★ ★

nearly thirty years on the third Friday in April. Owner Terry Clarke, who bought the place with a partner in 2005, is a local who still isn't sure why his bar is such a draw.

"You drive down, look at it, and say, 'Jeez, this is what everybody's talking about,'" he said. And yet, after a couple of hours, even the stone-cold sober are drinking in the laid-back vibe. A nearby military base may help, because those folks get stationed all over the world. The Tiki Bar opening is like a reunion, said Clarke. One couple who met at the bar in the 1980s returns every year to see their friends.

Or maybe the allure of opening day of an open-air bar is simple spring fever. A virulent strain often spreads after Maryland's often long spring tease.

The Tiki Bar's formal address is 81 Charles Street, but it's easy to simply drive into town and look for it on the right after the road bends left away from the water. More information can be found at www .tikibarsolomons.com.

Save It for Later
St. Leonard

If you dig a hole, what might you find? Perhaps a bodkin. Maybe some sprue. Seven million objects found in Maryland by archaeologists, going back 12,000 years, are housed at the Maryland Archaeological Conservation Laboratory at Jefferson Patterson Park, located at 10505 Mackall Road (410-586-8550; www.jefpat.org), and you, the touring public, can have a peek by appointment.

The "MAC Lab," as it's called, features the East Coast's largest archeological vacuum freeze dryer to chill out all those archaeological finds, such as petroglyphs dynamited in the 1920s from the Susque-hanna River cliffs to make way for the Conowingo Dam. There's the massive 22-foot paddlewheel from the steamship *Columbus* (which caught fire and sank off Baltimore in 1850), retrieved from Davy Jones's locker. A personal favorite is the original cypress acorn from atop the Maryland State House. According to the state archives, the acorn stood from the 1780s to 1996, through all kinds of weather. Covered in copper, it came down because it had rotted inside.

In addition to these marquee items, the MAC Lab holds onto the flotsam and jetsam of everyday life, like small, white Colonial wig curlers and mother lodes of stuff found at privy sites. Think about it. Due to soft landings, artifacts are relatively intact. Digs yield twentieth-century objects layered over those from older eras. Consider a black plastic pepper shaker, clearly a knockoff of the *Venus de Milo*. It was found under the floorboards of an old farmhouse. Kitschy, kitschy, but part of Maryland's official archeology record.

As for bodkins and sprue? The former is a thick needle that ladies used to thread ribbons through their corsets. The latter is waste metal, left over from castings.

This Little Light
St. Clements Island

The way the government went around automating old lighthouses years ago, you'd think the market for new ones had dried up. Well, you'd be wrong.

Down on St. Clements Island, where Maryland was born in 1634, workers spent nearly a year rebuilding a light that burned down in 1957. Locals missed the place. When a woman whose grandmother had been a lighthouse keeper in the mid-1800s died, she left a bequest and a request.

Named Josephine for her grandmother, the late benefactor had come to Dick Gass, president of St. Clement's Hundred, and told him: "I trust you. I'm going to leave you something. Do something on the island; remember my grandmother's work." She left $5,000, half her liquid assets.

One thing led to another, spurred by memories of the light. In came the grants and appropriations. Don Cropp, a local builder, saw that

The crowning touch is added to the rebuilt St. Clements Island light. COURTESY OF ST. MARY'S COUNTY MUSEUM DIVISION; GREG MORA, PHOTOGRAPHER

210 tons of sand and gravel, 45,000 bricks, and 4,000 blocks went to the island by barge. Local Amish milled loblolly pine. A building that originally cost $5,300 was reborn—to the tune of $600,000.

"If you look at it, it looks like the original. The windows have wavy glass. Porcelain knobs," said Cropp, who oversaw the construction project.

One April day when the water was calm, a barge traveled to the island with a big crane and a cupola to crown the lighthouse. No, the light doesn't light. But the lighthouse looks authentic, so it seems like it might.

Visit the lighthouse on summer weekends via ferry from the St. Clement's Island Museum, 38370 Point Breeze Road in Colton's Point. For details, call (301) 769-2222 or visit www.co.saint-marys.md.us/recreate/museums/stclementsisland.asp.

Lost and Found
St. Mary's City

A whole city hidden under a cornfield? It sounds like John Deere's version of Atlantis. It really happened, though, right here in Maryland.

Founded in 1634 and abandoned in 1695, Maryland's original capital city cooled its heels (so to speak) for almost 300 years before somebody came looking for it. Today, Historic St. Mary's City (HSMC) at 18550 Hogaboom Lane (800-762-1634; www.stmaryscity.org) is a living history and archaeology museum where seventeenth-century life is re-created even as it's being excavated.

Amazing what folks have looked for here. How about trapped seventeenth-century air? This was a tantalizing possibility back in the mid-1990s when three lead coffins were discovered during a dig. They were buried at a circa 1667 chapel, just the place to inter people rich enough to buy lead coffins.

In the end, the air was declared plain old 1990s air, but not before it was tested by no less an authority than NASA. I mean, this was a big

deal. The coffins' occupants turned out to be members of Maryland's founding Calvert family—Philip—his first wife, and an unidentified child. Today you can learn more about the coffins at the HSMC visitor center. And stay tuned, because the chapel is being rebuilt on its original 3-foot-wide by 5-foot-deep foundation. By the time it opens, an exact replica of the church's tabernacle (the wooden altarpiece) might be in place. The original was donated to Baltimore's Sisters of Mercy in the 1850s by descendants of Charles Carroll, a Maryland signer of the Declaration of Independence and member of a leading Catholic family here in a colony settled by Catholics searching for religious freedom. True fact: St. Mary's City was the first place in the British colonies to promote religious toleration.

The chapel is only one facet of early life found at Historic St. Mary's City. Visitors can see a tobacco farm; a replica of the *Dove,* which brought colonists across the Atlantic; and much more.

Ham It Up
St. Mary's County

Boston bakes its beans and Chicago deep-dishes pizza. Not to be outdone, Southern Maryland stuffs a corned ham with kale (and sometimes cabbage and onions). It's likely to dominate Thanksgiving tables in St. Mary's County, much as turkey rules elsewhere.

Sandwiches featuring the unlikely ham-kale combo line up alongside hot dogs and fried dough at festivals. You can even buy Southern Maryland ham sandwiches at a few places.

"Either you love it or hate it," said Gilbert Murphy, proprietor of the family-owned Murphy's Town & Country Store, which opened in 1949.

Known variously as Maryland Stuffed Ham or Southern Maryland Ham (and I've heard "kale-stuffed ham"), the dish seems indigenous to St. Mary's County, though it pops up in Calvert and Charles. It's not clear just who figured out how to put kale in a ham, but locals have been doing it forever.

"You remember the old black pots they cooked in? They didn't have a lot of room. Someone figured out to put it all in one big pot," said Virginia Tennyson. She learned the recipe from her grandmother and heard that the dish dates to Colonial times.

If you're traveling in the southernmost reaches of the Old Line State, look for stuffed ham sandwiches at Chaptico Market, 25466 Maddox Road in Chaptico (301-884-3308), or Murphy's Town & Country Store at 21270 Abell Road in Avenue (301-769-3131).

The Hatbox Splint
Waldorf

The tale of John Wilkes Booth has oft been told: how the actor plotted to kill president Abraham Lincoln, assassinated him at Ford's Theatre in Washington, D.C., and was on the run for more than a week before he was captured and killed in a Virginia barn.

Booth broke his leg after he leapt from the president's box seat that fateful April evening, and it was set later that night by a Charles County doctor named Samuel A. Mudd. It'll give you goose bumps to visit Mudd's home and climb the same staircase Booth did, which you'll do during a tour of the Dr. Samuel A. Mudd House at 3725 Dr. Samuel A. Mudd Road (310-645-6870; www.somd.lib.md.us/museums/mudd .htm). The house has regular hours on Wednesday, Saturday, and Sunday from late March to mid-late November.

As the story goes, Booth and an accomplice made it to Dr. Mudd's house about 4:00 a.m. the night of the assassination. In the dark, the two men at Dr. Mudd's door said that one had fallen from his horse. Booth wore a false beard. The doctor led Booth to a living room settee that remains today at the house. He then fetched a lamp, and the trio went upstairs to a bedroom where Dr. Mudd cut off Booth's boot and fixed him up with a split made from a wooden hatbox. By 4:00 p.m., the assassins were gone.

An 1865 dresser that was in the bedroom with Booth also remains.

So does the same wavy windowpane glass he would have looked out of, which struck me as positively spooky.

Dr. Mudd went on to imprisonment in the Dry Tortugas, where he helped cure a yellow fever epidemic. This led to his pardon by president Andrew Jackson. You'll have to do your own research to learn the details of this saga, including the fact that Dr. Mudd always maintained his innocence. At his home, I learned that his grandson spent eighty years trying to clear the good doctor's name.

The house, on 197 acres, is full of period furnishings, twenty-six items of which belonged to Dr. Mudd—including his medical case. Others have been collected from members of the family, which has been in the area since the 1600s.

5

Suburban Washington, D.C.

In Maryland's Washington, D.C., suburbs, it's hard to tell where one town ends and the next one begins. It's as if the suburbs have suburbs. Who drew the boundaries around here?

The countryside surrounding our nation's capital has many tales to tell. Early nineteenth-century politicians slipped over the D.C. border to Bladensburg, where they dueled to the death. In Bethesda, a home's log wing may well be the cabin that inspired Harriet Beecher Stowe's Uncle Tom's Cabin.

National treasures have spilled over the border into Maryland. In a small museum in Bowie stands an early remote-control system for a radio. College Park turns out to be quite the major home to early aviation. And I still can't picture one of its major firsts, the initial test-fire of a machine gun from an airplane.

Like suburbs everywhere, ours have grown. Please note that Frederick County, farm country with an eponymous historic city (where schools close for the Great Frederick Fair each fall), is in this chapter. The explanation? I followed the state tourism department's definition of the state's regions, only they call this the "Capital Region."

No question, the D.C. suburbs are full of bright and accomplished people. Don't talk politics with them unless you want to dig in like a scholar. The suit who seems to be talking to himself (Bluetooth is long in the tooth around here) or the pontificator in the local breakfast joint no doubt read and dissected the Washington Post before they brushed their teeth.

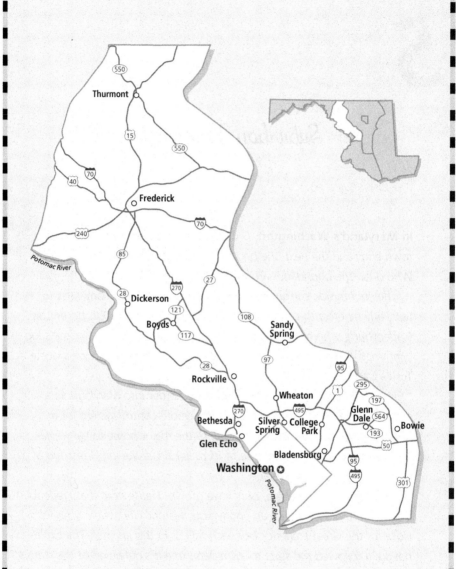

Suburban Washington, D.C.

An artist gives kids their storybook characters at the Dennis and Phillip Ratner Museum.

Of Mice and Moses

Bethesda

A haircut magnate and his artist-cousin have joined forces to bring you visual tours of the Old Testament *and* favorite fairy tales. Think of it as "Samson and Delilah meet Aladdin."

See them—and more—at the Dennis and Phillip Ratner Museum at 10001 Old Georgetown Road (301-897-1518; www.ratnermuseum .com). Dennis, a founder of the Hair Cuttery chain of salons, and his cousin Philip, a prolific sculptor, collaborated on the Israel Bible Museum in Safed, Israel, some years ago. In 2000 they opened this museum in their D.C.-area stomping grounds.

Philip sculpts wiry figures of biblical subjects from polyform clay over welded steel for his museum. On the second floor, about eighty

sculptures and fifty drawings depict the Old Testament. Eve seems to spring literally from Adam's rib. Noah, head back, sits atop a pyramid of twos: elephants, giraffes, camels, and . . . you know the rest. By the time Moses parts the sea, it looks as though the waves will turn back and crash over him.

"His idea in creating these Old Testament sculptures is, whether you're 5 or 105, to have a visual experience and get you thinking about the Bible," says Stella Bernstein, the museum's administrative director.

In a building behind the main museum filled with characters from children's literature, kids make art. Philip has designed an activity to go along with each of the characters marching through the room: Puss in Boots, Pinocchio, and even the Big Bad Wolf. Most of whom, when you think about it, star in tales that have morals with Biblical proportion.

Queen of the Avenue
Bethesda-Chevy Chase

Along Wisconsin Avenue, a major boulevard in and out of Washington, stand many upscale shopping haunts such as Dior, Saks, Jimmy Choo, and Tiffany & Co. You'll even find the National Institutes of Health, frequently in the news (well, that far north the road's name has changed to Rockville Pike, but you get the idea). This is hardly where you'd expect to find a salute to pioneer women. But there she stands, less than a mile from the medical complex, near the corner of Wisconsin Avenue and Montgomery Lane.

This is the twelfth and final Madonna of the Trail, one in a series of Madonnas erected by the Daughters of the American Revolution in the 1920s along the National Old Trails Road that stretches from coast to coast. If you look at her from one side, the old Bethesda Post Office makes for a nice period companion piece. From the other, the Hyatt reminds the viewer of the twentieth century. The twenty-first century is represented by a tattoo parlor around the corner.

A salute to pioneers stands in modern times. SARA MORELL

★ ★

A House by the Side of the Road

Bethesda

Astute readers may have noticed a few entries in this book that aren't quirky, offbeat, or funny. What they are: unique and unexpected, which qualifies them as a curiosity in my book.

So it goes for the small house with a log wing at 11420 Old Georgetown Road, which sits along a major commuter route through subdivisions convenient to the Beltway. With all the trees out front, you really can't see it from the road in summer. Believe it or not, the little log wing is thought to have been the inspiration for *Uncle Tom's Cabin,* by way of a slave's biography. Here's the story:

Reverend Josiah Henson, born in Charles County in 1789, lived on this property for most of 1795–1830. He grew to be much-trusted, even traveling to Kentucky with other slaves when owner Isaac Riley, nearing bankruptcy, engaged in nineteenth-century offshore bank accounting (so to speak) by hiding them at his brother's place there. The surprising part? Henson, a religious man of conscious, kept his word and didn't defect in slave-free Ohio. No, he returned to Riley's plantation.

Long story short: Riley then swindled Henson out of a deal to buy his freedom, leading to Henson's escape north to Canada. There, he established a community called Dawn and went on to a life of considerable note. He wrote an autobiography (and added to it five times over nearly thirty years), the first of which Harriet Beecher Stowe read. She then adapted portions of it into *Uncle Tom's Cabin,* the 1852 blockbuster novel that boosted the abolitionist movement and led Abraham Lincoln himself to call Stowe "the little lady that started the big war."

The house is plain inside, with wide plank floors indicating the portions that are likely to be original. This was the main house when a 500-acre plantation rolled across this part of suburbia. The log wing was slightly separate from the house during Henson's era, and is thought to have been the kitchen where Henson, in his autobiography, referenced sleeping one night. The original walls and fireplace still stand today.

Almost as surprising as the treasure this house may hold is the fact that it remained in private hands until 2006, when the local government bought it. Currently, it's known variously as the Josiah Henson Historic Site, Uncle Tom's Cabin, and/or the Riley House. Scholars are evaluating its architecture and studying the lives of Henson and his family, Riley and his family, and, no doubt, anyone else connected with the story. It's hoped that it will be regularly open to the public by 2012. Until then, keep an eye out for occasional openings, including during Montgomery County's late-June Heritage Days. Check www .josiahhensonsite.org for the latest.

Wired for Sound
Bowie

Back in the 1980s, remote controls began to proliferate and spread faster than excuses from politicians caught lying. No longer did parents warn Johnny to move back from the TV or ruin his eyesight. No, Dad had a new problem on his hands: He had to wrestle Johnny for his Barcalounger *and* his spiffy new giant-size TV remote.

Looking back, the arrival of this gadget could only have been part of the natural order. For evidence, you only need look to the Radio and Television Museum at 2608 Mitchellville Road (301-390-1020; www .radiohistory.org). On display there is the "Mystery Control," a handsome wood-veneer box the size of a medium bag of potato chips. It debuted in 1939, partnered with the Philco Model 39-116 radio. If you dial "8" on the control's Bakelite telephone dial, the big radio switches over to preprogrammed station #8. A guy barely had to lift his head from the antimacassar to switch from the game to *The Jack Benny Program.*

Housed in a 1905 farmhouse across from a 7-Eleven, the museum,

Off With Their Heads

Slipping over the border is a time-honored tactic among furtive deed-doers. That's why nineteenth-century congressmen took their grievances across the Washington, D.C., line into Maryland, where dueling was legal. The Bladensburg Dueling Grounds saw plenty of blood spilled during the century's first half.

It is said that twenty-six to fifty duels (but who's counting?) took place in the nondescript ravine near Fort Lincoln Cemetery on Route 450. The first congressmen pointed pistols on "the dark and bloody grounds" in 1808. Next up were Virginia cousins—one a senator—caught up in a squabble over a local election. The senator died.

The most famous duel happened in 1820, when James Barron faced off against Commodore Stephen Decatur over a nasty international incident. Barron had been court-martialed and lost command of the frigate *Chesapeake* after an 1807 encounter with the British. His surrender led to the War of 1812. (Side note for you history buffs: The redcoats arrived in Bladensburg, defeated local forces, then headed west to burn Washington, D.C., during that war.) Decatur sat on the board of inquiry that court-martialed Barron, and Barron went on to nurse an epic grudge that led to the March 22, 1820, duel. Decatur died in his Lafayette Square house in Washington. Barron recovered from his wounds, but never from the public scorn that followed.

The showdown that more or less put an end to the dueling ground came when Maine congressman Jonathan Cilley insulted a New York editor over an article he didn't like. His fellow congressman, William J. Graves of Kentucky, took up for the editor, and Cilley wound up dead. Dueling laws toughened up after that, although the occasional match still took place at Bladensburg up until the Civil War.

open Friday from 10:00 a.m. to 5:00 p.m. and Saturday and Sunday from 1:00 to 5:00 p.m., is far more sophisticated than one might suspect. See a few inches of the Atlantic cable used by telegraphs in the 1870s. Dig the "auto radio" made for Chrysler in 1935, a sizable model that managed to squeeze under the dash. The Crosley Model 118 Reado was the fax machine's forebear. Those still waiting for prices to drop on high-definition TVs will learn, yet again, that the more things change, the more they stay the same. For here you'll see the first mass-produced color television, the RCA Model CT-100. When introduced in 1954, it cost a cool $1,000.

Dairy King
Boyds

Deep in the heart of upscale suburbia stands some fancy recreational stuff, such as a SoccerPlex and a Splash Playground. Plus, of course, subdivisions with lawns carved from former farm fields.

Once upon a time—and not so long ago—wheat, oats, hay, and corn grew on this real estate. So did dairies. A stone's toss from the water playground stands an old barn, built in 1930, that's being turned into a dairy "mooseum."

As Shakespeare said, what is past is prologue. Apparently, the cows did pretty well in Montgomery County, where 300 dairies operated at the height of its bovine abundance in 1952.

At the King Barn Dairy Mooseum (www.mooseum.com), see a calf's nursing bottle, which, trust me, is bigger than the one your mother used for you. Cow milkers emerge from a round metal disc. Inside the barn, white metal pipes that delineated cow stalls line each side of the building. An acrylic, milkable cow is on the way, which will give kids a real-life experience without the cleanup. Best of all, descendants of dairy families are donating heirlooms, like big metal milk cans. So the mooseum's bringing folks together, like a big Maryland dairy family reunion.

★ ★

Currently, the fledgling mooseum works with a nearby school and is open for such events as Montgomery County's Heritage Days at the end of June, and the Farm Tour weekend at the end of July. Limited weekend hours are anticipated by 2010. Look for the wooden Holstein cow out front when the barn is open at 18028 Central Park Circle, South Germantown Recreational Park, or contact them at (301) 528-6530 or dairymooseum@aol.com.

Key's Chain

The pride of Maryland, "Star-Spangled Banner" composer Francis Scott Key, turns up all over the Free State. In Frederick, the town where he was born and is buried, they've named the local Class A baseball team, the mall, and even a car dealership for our bard. In Annapolis, the auditorium at Key's alma mater, St. John's College, is named for him but the whole building in which it resides is known as "FSK."

Most Marylanders probably think they know all they need to know about Key. (After all, how much do you really need to know?) In researching this book, I digested some juicy tidbits that may have passed folks by.

- It's well-known that Key wrote the "Star-Spangled Banner" from a ship in the Patapsco River while watching the bombs bursting in air above Baltimore's Fort McHenry. The question is, what was he doing there? We know why the British were there. They invaded in 1814. But Scott was an attorney. Here's a morsel for your next cocktail party: Key was rescuing an Upper Marlboro man, Dr. William Beanes, who'd gotten tangled up with the British. Seems

Props

College Park

College Park, home to the University of Maryland, may seem an odd choice for an aviation museum. But aviation dawned at its airport in 1909. Honest. Under contract from the feds, the brothers Wright sold the U.S. government its first "aeoroplane," and Wilbur showed up soon after to teach two guys to fly it. An Army Aviation School opened in 1911.

they stopped at his home on their march to burn Washington and complications ensued, so they decided to hold him aboard British Admiral Cochrane's flagship.

- FSK's teenage son Daniel was killed at the Bladensburg Dueling Grounds. His fellow midshipman and bunkmate John Sherburne won the argument, which stemmed from a disagreement over the speed of steamboats. At least it wasn't about girls, like his brother. Read on.

- FSK lost son Philip Barton Key after Key the younger apparently cuckolded a New York congressman. And not just any ole U.S. representative. Daniel E. Sickles, acquitted of shooting the younger Key by reason of insanity, went on to become a controversial Union general a few years later. Sickles murdered Key, the U.S. Attorney for Washington, across from the White House.

- Author F. Scott Fitzgerald's full name is Francis Scott Key Fitzgerald due to a family tie on his father's side. Fitzgerald, with Montgomery County connections, is buried in Rockville. Read all about it in the "At Rest" entry in this chapter.

★ ★

The first helicopter to achieve vertical flight is displayed in College Park.

Over the next two years came other firsts: the first bomb-dropping device tested from an airplane, the first machine gun shots tested from an airplane, and the first mile-high flight. All of this is chronicled at the College Park Aviation Museum, located at 1985 Corporal Frank Scott Drive (301-864-6029; www.collegeparkaviationmuseum.com).

By the time inventor Emile Berliner and his son, Henry, started their flight tests on the very first helicopter to achieve vertical flight in 1924, the U.S. Postal Air Mail Service was taking off from College Park. The Berliner plane's successful test flight was achieved with a version of the craft that had triple-layer wings. This increased the plane's lift as it moved forward. It also had stronger engines than previous tests, thanks to a highly interested U.S. Navy. By the time the flight ended, the craft had reached an altitude of 15 feet and a speed of 40 miles per hour, and it had maneuvered a radius of 150 feet.

The helicopter we know today emerged in 1940, constructed by Igor Sikorsky. So, while the Berliner flight is a first, the senior Berliner's more enduring legacy may be Nipper, the RCA-Victor dog, trademarked from a painting for the Berliner Gramophone Co. The company was sold in 1900 and re-named Victor Records. You probably know the rest of the story.

A Menagerie

Dignitaries collect all kinds of stuff while globe-trotting, and disgraced vice president Spiro Agnew was no different. Lucky Maryland—some of his booty ended up at the University of Maryland archives. Specifically, it's on top of a map/filing cabinet, in an archival box. There, carefully preserved, is a monkey fur cape presented to the vice president in 1971 by Kenya's first president and prime minister, Jomo Kenyatta.

Why monkey fur? Or a cape? Those details have been lost to time. The cape certainly adds a unique touch to the official White House photo of the Agnew-Kenyatta meeting that's also part of the Agnew Papers. Perhaps it was something uniquely Kenyan circa 1971. Another tidbit: The cape was treated with DDT, though who knows why. The poison pesticide was banned in the U.S. before Agnew resigned in 1973 under criminal investigation for federal tax evasion. In 1974 most of his papers came here. (Did you know he was once Baltimore County Executive?) Agnew always maintained his innocence, and died in 1996.

As for the monkey fur cape, it is stored next to an archival box containing another Agnew animal mystery—a zebra skin rug. Says Jennie Levine, curator for historical manuscripts: "We definitely don't know where that came from."

★ ★

Churning through the Years

College Park

Maryland is a hotbed for ice cream. Who knew? Baltimore dairyman Jacob Fussell invented commercial ice-cream production in 1851. University of Maryland professor Wendell Arbuckle studied his way around the stuff's crystalline structure and became the "Father of Modern Ice Cream." And Arbuckle's employer, the University of Maryland, has produced its own ice cream since 1924. (Should we call Maryland the "Birthplace of the Freshman 15"?)

Since the university started as an agriculture school, with its own dairy and cows, it's a no-brainer why ice-cream making is part of the school's heritage. Final Exam Cram (cappuccino with chocolate cookie pieces) and numerous other flavors issue daily from the university's ice-cream-making machine. Even better, you can try them. The dairy is in Turner Hall, also the campus visitor center, and worth a stop for something cool and sweet. It's open Monday through Friday, 10:00 a.m. to 4:00 p.m., but you might want to check hours during school breaks.

For years, the urban myth has floated around that the ice cream's fat content is so high, you can't sell it off campus. Not true. Also not true (but *soo* D.C.) is the rest of the story that says the FDA is trying to shut down the operation. Enough about rumors—let's eat. I can vouch for the Fear the Turtle flavor, a white chocolate with pecans and a caramel so creamy, you'd swear they just scooped it from the vat.

Fear the Turtle

College Park

True confession from a Marylander whose family ties go back three whole generations (itself a curiosity in the state's transitory suburban region): First time I saw the University of Maryland's slogan—on a ball cap while Christmas shopping—I laughed. Scrawled across the top: "Fear the Turtle."

Life provides plenty to fear. The reaper, for one. Big dogs with bared teeth. But a turtle?

You'd better believe it. The University of Maryland's athletic battle cry, coined by a student in 1989, has taken the Free State by storm. The academic end of the institution has also embraced the slogan, and the university has officially copyrighted "Fear the Turtle." As the school's marketing director says, it's "extremely unique" to Maryland.

"Some people don't get it, but that's OK," a UM official said. "They're curious to learn more." And that, for a marketing campaign, is the goal entirely. To hear the turtle roar: www.feartheturtle.umd .edu/stuff.

All Hail

College Park

Hulking football players rumbling toward the gridiron stop and rub his shiny bronze beak. Fretful freshmen and skating-by sophomores bring him offerings: a muffin, a candle, or just a "please-*please*" plea when exam week arrives. He's Testudo, the terrapin who reigns over the University of Maryland. Students depend on him for good luck.

Parked in front of the centrally located McKeldin Library, Testudo the bronze sculpture surveys his kingdom. Like most rulers, he is not alone. There's a Testudo at Byrd Stadium, one at the Riggs Alumni Center, and even a taxidermy specimen stored in the university archives. He was the model when big bronze Testudo was made, back when our story began.

Once upon a time, the University of Maryland's athletic teams were called the Old Liners. Even though George Washington supposedly dubbed Maryland the "Old Line State," in 1932 the editors of the school newspaper, *The Diamondback,* wanted a name change. Football coach Dr. H. "Curley" Byrd helpfully hailed from deep in the heart of Maryland's Eastern Shore, where diamondback turtles remained plentiful. Byrd, who went on to become the school's president, secured the terrapin as school mascot.

★ ★

Testudo the terrapin oversees the College Park campus of the University of Maryland. The ice cream is made at the school.

Testudo the bronze terrapin was unveiled in 1933. First installed at Ritchie Coliseum, Testudo—whose name may stem from Testudines, the scientific classification for turtle—has overlooked McKeldin Mall since the 1960s.

Rollin' on the River

Dickerson

Confederate General Jubal Early gave 'em hell around here during the Civil War, then turned around and gave 'em hell when he got back home. He refused to pledge allegiance to the Union after the war. During the war Early crossed the Potomac River just north of White's Ferry. So, R. Edwin Brown decided to name his ferry after the guy.

Every unflooded, unfrozen day for the last umpteen generations, a ferry has trundled back and forth across the Potomac River here, linking Maryland to Virginia. Commuters attempting to outwit the region's gridlocked interstates find their way to the landing, where 160 cars per hour cross aboard the *General Jubal A. Early.* Should you arrive as the cable ferry is pulling away from the riverbank, your wait lasts only twelve to fifteen minutes. Trust me, it's a far more serene twelve to fifteen minutes than those you'd spend stuck on nearby Interstate 270.

Ferry operators live at the landing. Living by the ferry sounds romantic until you try it. Brown, whose grandson oversees operations, called the Potomac "a wild river" and he should know. In 1946, when he and his one-time partners bought the ferry, they reestablished service that had been swept away by a 1942 flood. The water hasn't quit rising. "We've had two massive floods in the last fifty years," says Brown. An elaborate effort involving pumps and a tractor affixed to the ferry keeps the boat from sinking—or from getting swept away.

Because you can't fool Mother Nature, when the river floods commuters have to wait until the waters recede. But they don't seem to mind. White's Ferry is the last ferry left on the Potomac River. For more information, call (301) 349-5200 or visit www.historicwhitesferry.com. For directions, try entering "White's Ferry, MD" into your destination on www.mapquest.com.

Do No Harm

Frederick

Deep in the heart of Frederick lies a place with a past where nineteenth-century furniture makers once worked. What with their carpentry, aka coffin-making, skills, these men often held a second job as the local undertaker. Business picked up significantly during the nearby Civil War campaigns, especially Antietam, the nation's bloodiest day. As a result, yet another practice was called into service at 48 East Patrick Street: An embalmer set up shop.

Remarkably, the folks who established the National Museum of Civil War Medicine knew nothing of the building's parallel past when plans to move into the former furniture makers' first developed. But they've made up for lost time. On the first floor, a display reflects the building's grim past with an "ice coffin." When filled with ice, its reusable metal tray kept bodies cool until they were embalmed or buried. In the fall of 1862, after Antietam, the ice coffin stayed full. Five of the coffins were brought to Frederick after the battle, according to museum director George Wunderlich. "Most guys were buried on the battlefield," he said.

The museum also documents major medical advances that took place during the war. The tibia and fibula of soldiers such as twenty-year-old Bartholomew Fields of Lenoir County, North Carolina, are here. That's because the bones of men who were operated on were saved for study—a valuable teaching tool for young doctors of the day.

A nineteenth-century drug chest bears mercurial ointments and bicarbonate of soda, aka Alka Seltzer. Some things just don't change.

In addition to the Frederick location, Civil War medical tales are told by the museum at a second location. The Pry House Field Hospital Museum is located at Antietam National Battlefield, and is open seasonally. You can contact the museum at (301) 695-1864 or go to www.civilwarmed.org for more information.

Fooling Yourself or Fooling Nobody?

Frederick

Artists see inspiration everywhere. A dull cement bridge over a creek in the middle of Frederick, for instance.

Artist William Cochran painted the bridge so now it looks like it's made of stone. Not only that, but one with birds, ivy, and all kinds of other symbols. The Community Bridge between East Patrick and East All Saints Streets was painted in the trompe l'oeil style, which means "deceive the eye." What you see is not necessarily what you get.

Is this Frederick landmark real or is it faux?

"It's a metaphor," says Cochran. "I think that the bridge is all about the connections between people that are often invisible to us."

An expansive community process came into play soon after Cochran got the idea to paint the bridge. He and his wife, Teresa, elicited ideas for design elements, aka symbols, that local folks consider community-related. One woman suggested a spider web because delicate strands combine into something strong and flexible. Somebody else came up with a cup of coffee. That's neighborly.

This all unfolded a decade ago and since then, birds have been spotted trying to land at the trompe l'oeil fountain. Swaggering teens have been overheard saying "Betcha I can move that sculpture," which, of course, is painted on the bridge.

In the end, the bridge's thin layer of paint fools the eye the same way that people's surface differences fool one another.

★ ★

Chicken Noodle Soup and Candy Globes

Frederick

Nancy Watt's been waiting tables at the Barbara Fritchie Candy Stick Restaurant since 1967. Her advice to new owners who've arrived on her watch is simple: Don't change the chicken noodle soup, keep the multicolored Danish light fixtures (aka "candy globes"), and do not mess with the turkey that is much beloved in open-faced sandwiches. These are pillars of the home-cooking dished up for decades at this restaurant on U.S. Highway 40 west as you travel out of town. Look for the giant candy cane out front. In a pinch, call (301) 662-2500.

The real Barbara Fritchie was a Frederick woman who died soon after the Civil War. John Greenleaf Whittier memorialized her in what may be an apocryphal poem that celebrated her Union patriotism. Her house, located at 154 West Patrick Street in downtown Frederick (301-698-8992), is open to the public and part of her legend. Decades ago, the Candystick restaurant started out nearby, and they even made candy there back then. It later moved out to US 40.

John Burner bought the restaurant with partners a couple of years back, repainted the big candy cane, and plans to keep the building's red, white, and blue decor outside. As he points out, even if the poem is lore, "it still shows a ninety-something lady who got up and defended her flag and country."

Time Travel

Glenn Dale

During a single spring weekend, Romans in Mohawk helmets meet Vietnam War vets as Confederate and Union soldiers ponder foxholes dug by World War II American servicemen. Really.

Time's no longer a continuum during Marching Through Time, a weekend gathering that draws reenactors from every era you can think of. Talk about "living history"! Men and women have emerged to represent the Hundred Years' War, the Napoleonic Wars, and even the

To find Barbara Fritchie's Candy Stick Restaurant, look for the giant candy cane.

Bronze Age. Sounds like tutors everywhere need to bring their struggling history students. You can check it out the second weekend of April at the Marietta Mansion, 5626 Bell Station Road, or learn more about the event by calling (301) 464-5291 or consulting www.pgparks .com.

Behind the wool coat of a reenactor, you're likely to find a student of military history whose "impression"—or uniform and accompanying gear—is as authentic as modern times can muster. Reenactors interested in more recent times, like World War II, find a resource the Civil War reenactors never did, and that's genuine veterans. During a past Marching Through Time, reenactors learned their digs were too fancy because they were corrected by veterans of the Greatest Generation's war. During the war, soldiers slept in holes on the battlefield. In trees. In barns. Often, they hadn't slept in a tent since basic training.

Sounds realistic, doesn't it? As convincing as finding out that even in April, chain mail gets hot. Just ask somebody from medieval times.

A Penny Saved
Glen Echo

Clara Barton, the Civil War–era "Angel of the Battlefield," lived in one heck of a unique house. It's a rambling Victorian built especially for her, located in a notably sylvan neighborhood.

The home at 5801 Oxford Road was payment to her for lending her fame and expertise to the new Glen Echo development. The idea was for Clara, founder of the American Red Cross, to serve on the Women's Executive Committee of a soon-to-fail educational venture attached to the development.

Instead, Clara ended up using the stone house as a Red Cross warehouse. When she later decided to move in, it was renovated and doubled as the Red Cross headquarters. In fact, where Miss Barton ended and the Red Cross began became a smudged point of internal conflict that led to her departure. But for quite a few years, the house was more or less "Camp Red Cross." Volunteers from around the country

Clara Barton's clever house reflects her U.S. Red Cross roots, what with the muslin covering the walls.

stayed in one of ten second-floor bedrooms. They bustled through the front hall, with its unusual central section opened up to the third floor, and worked at four wooden desks in a back office.

Miss Barton herself sat at a rolltop desk in the back hallway. Her backless cane chair carries its own undocumented and perhaps apocryphal story: that Miss Barton whacked off the back to emphasize a strident, slack-free work ethic. Stiff upper back, you might say.

★ ★

The building's closets held supplies, like blankets and cotton muslin used to make bandages. Look closely at the walls and ceilings of the house, and check out the long white band from which the central lamp hangs. Why, it's cotton muslin! Wasn't Clara clever? She used what she had when she fashioned muslin over beams and painted it. All, it is said, to save money.

To find out more about the Clara Barton National Historic Site, call (301) 320-1410 or visit http://home.nps.gov/clba.

Sanctum Sanctorum
Glen Echo

Deep on Mongolia's cold and breezy steppes, nomads live in circular structures of fabric and frame. They're called yurts, and the earthy structures morphed into an alternative housing option in the early 1970s. You may recall that was back when the environmental move-ment was newly under way and "green" still referred to dollar bills.

That's right about the time six yurts were built at the by-then-defunct Glen Echo Amusement Park. Apparently they were supposed to be part of a big happening on the National Mall in Washington, D.C. Instead, they became a pottery school, and signaled the park's rebirth as an arts center.

Today, the yurts are one of too few places around super-serious Washington that encourage a great big grin. Grab a tree-limb handle, pull open the wood door, step inside, and you'll see what I mean. They have corrugated pine ceilings, perhaps a Plexiglas skylight, and a coziness that makes a long winter bearable. Two cables and gravity's tension hold each yurt together, explains Jeff Kirk, who runs Glen Echo Pottery. The largest of the six houses the gallery.

Glen Echo Amusement Park had a long history that generations of Washingtonians recall. After one season as a Chautauqua Assembly—an arts and learning center—Glen Echo moved into its amusement park era in 1899. The park's popularity peaked during World War II, and it closed in 1968. Operated during its heyday as a "trolley park" by the Washington Railway and Electric Company (to boost earnings for the line that ended there), the place is still renowned for its Dentzel carousel. The historic carousel has been operating, with some time out for facelifts, since 1921.

From ballroom dancing to theater groups and more, Glen Echo has regained new life. The yurts, meantime, stand where the roller coaster once ruled. The park is at 7300 MacArthur Boulevard. For more info, call (301) 634-2222 or go to www.glenechopark.org.

At Rest

Rockville

Having fox-trotted their way through the United States and Europe during their prime, the leading lights of the Jazz Age came to rest in peace in the heart of suburbia, a stone's throw from one of the county's busiest intersections. Francis Scott Key Fitzgerald—known informally as F. Scott—had long visited the family farm at Rockville. (Yes, he was distantly related to the Marylander who wrote the national anthem.) Later in life, Fitzgerald rented a Towson estate when his wife, Zelda, was institutionalized at nearby Sheppard Pratt. Fitzgerald's estate was near present-day Towson University. More importantly, he wrote *Tender Is the Night* there.

Upon his death on December 21, 1940, at the age of forty-four, he was brought home to Rockville and interred in the Rockville Union Cemetery. When Zelda died in a sanitarium fire in North Carolina in 1948, she was buried there with her husband. The couple's only child, daughter Frances ("Scottie"), along with the ladies of the Women's Club of Rockville, were instrumental in moving the pair in 1975 to the Fitzgerald family plot at the historic St. Mary's Cemetery, 520 Veirs Mill Road.

Scottie, too, is now buried there.

★ ★

A Patriotic Pup and a Patriotic Man
Sandy Spring

When the green metal dog bed came up on eBay, Delmas Wood faced a quandary: Eight hundred dollars for Fala's little nest? He consulted his brother—a banker—who told him, "There's no price on history."

Five thousand dollars later, the dog bed of Franklin D. Roosevelt's fabled Scottie rests in the FDR Museum behind Wood's house at 7515 Dr. Bird Road, a humble locale full of hope, heart, and a lot of good stories. The dog bed, subject of a limited-edition print that proved to be popular when the Scottie Breeders' Association convened in Frederick one year, may be the museum's most tangible link to the late president's personal life. Well, not counting his Thermos, which he had left on a train.

Not only does Wood run his little museum (open by appointment, 301-924-0130), he also gives performances and talks on the Great Depression/World War II–era president and gives the proceeds to charity. They started when he entered a public-speaking contest. Almost by chance, he settled on Roosevelt's declaration-of-war speech. Wood went on to win the contest—more than once—and plays Roosevelt to the hilt, down to the metal leg braces.

Wood's FDR Museum includes a World War II room. Here you'll find a photo of the bomber *Memphis Belle* given to Wood by her captain, Robert Morgan. Even tougher to wrap your mind around: an autographed photo of one Fred J. Olivi, the co-pilot who dropped the bomb on Nagasaki, the earth-shattering event that helped end World War II. Olivi was a mere twenty-three when he flew that mission. It was his first.

Cheeburger, Cheeburger
Silver Spring

With the Hot Shoppes gone to hamburger heaven, local Marylanders flock to the Tastee Diners. Lucky us, we can choose from three. One is in Bethesda, one is in Laurel, and one is in Silver Spring, a location that proved to be so beloved that it was elevated to Montgomery County Historic Landmark status.

The diners go back to the 1930s. The original Silver Spring Tastee Diner was one of those places where some people showed up for all three meals and the waitresses knew what they wanted to eat. Then came redevelopment. Their favorite diner threatened, the locals mounted a mighty defense. Hearings convened. Tears streamed down cheeks as folks testified. "Save Our Diner" T-shirts appeared on city streets. The upshot? As a band played on, the diner was loaded onto a great big flatbed truck and moved three blocks down Georgia Avenue to 8601 Cameron Street. So you can still catch those blue plate specials, 24/7, Salisbury steak and all.

To find out more, call (301) 589-8171 or visit www.tasteediner.com.

From Mighty Oaks
Silver Spring

I'm not sure how you'd confirm it, but the giant acorn in Silver Spring seems to be the nation's largest. "I certainly haven't heard nor seen that any other town in America has a giant, inverted acorn," says Jerry McCoy, president of the Silver Spring Historical Society. Have you?

Locals spend a lot of time explaining that their town is called Silver *Spring*, not Silver *Springs*. Apparently a single spring, speckled with mica, was discovered here in 1840 by Francis Preston Blair, a major landowner with a very old Maryland name. The big acorn is a gazebo that sits above the spring, constructed in 1850 on Blair's estate.

There are two versions of the story, depending on which branch of the family is talking, says McCoy. The upshot, however, remains the same. Today, the giant acorn looks like it's holding off development, squeezed, as it is, into the urban intersection of East-West Highway and Newell Street. So, while I sit in traffic waiting for the light to change, it's nice to imagine this was once an estate on what must have been lovely rolling land.

A mighty acorn left over from a mighty estate stands in downtown Silver Spring.

A dining room's holiday tradition hangs over many a holiday luncheon.

Home for Christmas

Silver Spring

Hair bows. Starched calico skirts. They're gone, baby, gone. The waitresses at Mrs. K's Toll House haven't worn those outfits for a decade. The handiwork of waitresses past, however, is part of a holiday staple at the venerable restaurant, where the Christmas decor is an institution.

Back in the day, the waitresses made decorations. Some still hang at one end of the "Ben Franklin" dining room, a collection of old Styrofoam balls covered in sequins and velvet ribbon like everybody used to make for the tree. Slathering the main dining room's ceiling is a newer vintage of glass ornaments. Red, blue, Santa . . . even a glass rubber chicken (a cheeky waiter's contribution?). It's beautiful.

Alas, the plywood Santa and reindeer who ruled the roof for decades have been dispatched to the great toy shop in the sky. Still, this former tollhouse at 9201 Colesville Road (301-589-3500; www.mrsks.com), opened as Mrs. K's in 1930, retains its devotees who visit during the holidays to see those ornaments hanging from the dining room ceiling. Look for them starting the Monday after Thanksgiving, where they'll remain until January's half over.

Media Center

Thurmont

Here's a world-class curiosity: Winston Churchill played a jukebox in tiny Thurmont, Maryland. If only we knew what songs he played. Was he a Benny Goodman guy, or did he did he dig Cab Calloway?

Alas, that detail is lost to time but, as the politicos and media types say, make no mistake: The Cozy Restaurant & Inn knows. Located at 103 Frederick Road (301-271-7373; www.cozyvillage.com), "the Cozy" served Churchill that day. He was among the first of many dignitaries and other Washington types who've been there.

The restaurant/inn started in 1929 when Jerry Freeze's father set up a few tents, a gas station, and a camp stove in the Catoctin Mountains. The presidential connections began right away, since one of his customers turned out to be Herbert Hoover's secretary. That was before FDR dubbed a nearby retreat Shangri-La, which Eisenhower renamed Camp David in honor of his grandson. Then, the Cozy became headquarters for traveling press, U.S. State Department types, and the occasional presidential family member, appointee, or foreign dignitary in town for a summit.

"We had the Cronkites, the Brinkleys, and the Donaldsons," says Freeze. "That was years ago, when there were more large summits."

FDR is the only president to have visited the Cozy; the Secret Service nixed a Nixon trip. Back then, the press often stayed at the inn. "They were broadcasting from here and everything else at that time," says Freeze, whose Cozy Inn catering van has been spotted near Camp

David in television news clips. The Russian delegation visited the restaurant and left behind vodka, caviar, and a key to Russia—no small potatoes during the Cold War.

These days, the State Department gets first dibs on the inn's rooms and the White House press corps tends to stay at a nearby camp. The Cozy caters for them.

Given these kinds of connections—and years' worth of them—the Cozy has started a Camp David Museum in the restaurant to corral and display its memorabilia. Photographs, articles, drawings—you name it. The Cozy also has an inn, where the rooms are named for presidents. The Kennedy Room (actually, an executive suite) is the only one with a bidet.

Ugly Ducklings

Wheaton

It's odd to look at a beautiful swallowtail and know that it emerged from an ugly caterpillar. A really ugly one: The swallowtail's caterpillar looks, literally, like bird droppings. The white and brown caterpillar, you see, is wearing cammo, a shield against birds or any other predator that might be searching for supper. Clever, isn't it?

You can see the swallowtail in both its forms at Brookside Gardens' annual Wings of Fancy extravaganza, a butterfly show that runs May through October and is open daily. And it is a show.

The caterpillars stay in a small exhibit apart from the fabulosity flying about in the main building, the gardens' south conservatory at 1500 Glenallen Avenue (301-962-1453; www.mc-mncppc.org/parks/brookside). Upwards of 1,000 butterflies from 85 species swan about their glass house, showing off their blue, orange, and other ethereal hues on their gossamer wings. Tropical species sip from flower nectar; others prefer overripe fruit supplied by a friendly local produce market. Watermelon is a huge favorite, and the butterflies once got so excited about a raspberry puree that they flung it all over their greenhouse, just like toddlers at a spaghetti bowl.

Butterflies are free every summer at Brookside Gardens. BROOKSIDE GARDENS

The U.S. Department of Agriculture tightly regulates the butterflies in order to control the spread of parasites and disease. The packaging they arrive in as pre-caterpillar pupae gets dunked in a bleach solution to kill parasites and bacteria. And somebody always guards the greenhouse doors because it's the only way to ensure no butterfly hitchhikes to freedom on a visitor's shoulder.

6

Western Maryland

If somebody told me that Western Maryland considered itself a kind of "Maryland curiosity," I wouldn't be too surprised. Especially the part west of Hagerstown. Folks in this part of the state tend to look to Pittsburgh, not Maryland's usual Baltimore or Washington, D.C., as the "local" reference city. After all, the Free State narrows to a panhandle as it heads west and is only 2 miles wide at the town of Hancock.

Hills roll and mountains peak. Western Maryland is the kind of place where a couple of guys discover they both have draft horses. Well-trained woodsmen or artists fire up the chain saw to carve bears from fallen trees. A couple looking to launch a new business based on their love of dogsledding decided to open in Garrett County. Why? It gets an average 17 more inches of snow than Fairbanks, Alaska.

If I had to guess, I'd say the rest of the state doesn't know a whole heck of a lot about Western Maryland. At least, not those who don't have second homes at Deep Creek Lake or a family member at Frostburg State University. A buddy of mine packs a pet peeve about this: When she wants to know what the "DCL" weather's like, she can't get a decent forecast from her local Washington, D.C., weather guy. "The closest forecast comes out of Pittsburgh, and that's two hours away from Deep Creek!" she exclaimed.

Note to Maryland area big-city forecasters: Let's have the Garrett County forecast!

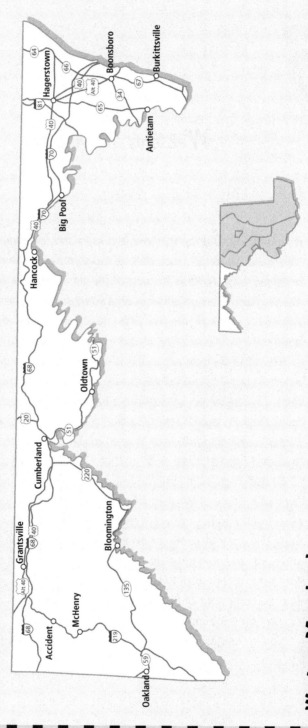

Western Maryland

One of the team at Husky Power Dogsledding in Accident guards his treasured possession.

Snow or No Snow: Mush!

Accident

According to the *American Heritage Dictionary* (and even my old *Oxford American Dictionary*), you'll find the word "mush" means to travel across snow with a dogsled. What they don't tell you is that you can also do this at 7:00 a.m. on a misty, 60-degree morning in Western Maryland. Who knew?

What may be North America's southernmost dogsledding tour company resides in the woods outside tiny Accident, where a retired Marine colonel and his artist-wife keep their windows open at night. Why? So they'll know if any of their dogs start to fret. You never know when a busy young dog named Smokey might start rattling his beloved food bowl. Fingers crossed that the yard's nine-year-old matriarch, a

How Accident Got Its Name

Some Maryland towns have funny names. One is Accident, in Garrett County. From various sources, here's what I know about how the town got its name:

King George paid off a debt to a fellow named George Deakins in about 1750. This was 600 acres in Western Maryland, which Deakins apparently got to choose himself. He sent out two survey parties to pick the best plot, but didn't tell either about the other. Will wonders never cease? Both parties picked the same 600 acres. They even marked the same tree as their starting tract. Ergo, this became known as the "Accident Tract," before it was Accident, Maryland.

In case you're wondering, the town's oldest known structure is the Drane House, built in 1797.

blonde Alaskan husky named ZsaZsa, will hush him before any humans awake. She may not call "haw" for left, or "gee" for right, or even "whoa." Still, ZsaZsa's a "leader," the alpha dog who keeps the others in line when they're harnessed to a sled (in snow) or wheeled cart (no snow). That's when they show their passengers what they're bred to do: run, run, run and pull, pull, pull. Groups and visitors can take short rides or longer runs, and tour the kennels.

Why Maryland? After retiring from military life, Mike and Linda Herdering traveled North America for two years in an RV to learn more about their longtime passion. Now settled near Deep Creek Lake (and Maryland native Linda's alma mater, Frostburg State University), Husky Power Dogsledding, at 2008 Bumble Bee Road (310-746-7200; www .huskypowerdogsledding.com), takes advantage of Western Maryland's annual snowfall that averages 100 inches. Come early June, rides are taken early in the day to accommodate the huskies. Let's remember that these friendly, well-trained dogs are used to running when the thermometer hovers around zero degrees Fahrenheit.

When not yelling "mush" or caring for their brood of fifteen to twenty dogs, the Herderings speak to school and civic groups about what they know best—mushing, and the care and training of their dogs.

A Passage to Cumberland
Allegany County

In the far wilds of Western Maryland stands a tunnel named for a weird fruit. The tunnel used to scare the heck out of mules. Once, a boss man had to smoke out two other guys who had a standoff in there. You? You should bring a flashlight if you visit the narrow Paw Paw Tunnel, part of the 184.5-mile-long Chesapeake & Ohio Canal, now a national park (www.nps.gov/choh), which follows alongside the Potomac River.

The tunnel was conceived as a way to skirt 6 winding miles at the river's Paw Paw Bends. Builders who tackled the tunnel between 1836 and 1850 quickly learned that blasting through a mountain had its issues. So did hauling 5.8 million bricks to the tunnel's remote location 25 miles (by modern highway) from Cumberland. Construction lasted twelve years beyond the original two-year forecast. Along the way came pestilence: cholera, money troubles, and serious labor problems that included feuds among immigrant workers who imported their differences from across the pond. Add the C&O Canal's race with the B&O Railroad for transportation supremacy, and it's a miracle the tunnel was ever built.

Once it opened, trouble continued because only one canal boat could pass through the tunnel at a time. Look for rope burns on old timber guardrails if you visit the 5/8-mile-long Paw Paw Tunnel, where a campground and picnic area stand nearby today. It's located near the town of Paw Paw, West Virginia, and you can find a map of the park at the C&O Canal website.

★ ★

An Apparition
Antietam

There's nothing funny about what happened on September 17, 1862. It remains the bloodiest day in U.S. military history when, during the Battle of Antietam near Sharpsburg, 23,000 were killed, wounded, or went missing.

Left behind, naturally, are the ghostly tales. Folks don't necessarily rest in peace near the battlefield. Among the stories floating around is one about a woman at the Otto House, which was used as a hospital after the war. A park ranger who wishes to remain anonymous confirmed his story to me as shared in *Ghosts of Antietam*, by Wilmer McKendree Mumma.

While securing the park at closing, right around twilight, Ranger A and Ranger B parked at the Otto House and decided to take an evening run along the Burnside Bridge. Off they went, and as they jogged back to their truck, the men spotted an apparition that scared the bejabbers out of them. They sprinted away from the house. Both had seen a woman in a hoop skirt in the doorway. Once they pulled themselves together, the duo made it back to their truck and skedaddled outta there. They didn't tell a soul for weeks until they overheard some workers complaining about spooky vibes at the Otto House. Then they started hearing about others who'd seen the woman.

Seems there may be a lady in a hoop skirt spending time at the Otto House, whether you believe in specters or not.

Open Exposure
Big Pool

Six miles west of Hancock, Sideling Hill gave travelers trouble for a *long* time. Stagecoaches crashed along the National Road. A hairpin curve on old U.S. Highway 40 (aka the old National Road) later caused nasty car accidents.

In the 1980s, in an effort to provide safer travel, builders blasted through the formidable hill to build Interstate 68, now the main road through Western Maryland. Check out the show-stopping rock formation here. It illustrates how, 250 million years ago, the Appalachian Mountains emerged after the North American and African continents collided to form a single continent called Pangaea. Geologists call the U-shaped formation a syncline, in which the U-shaped rock layers are evident. The opposite is an anticline, shaped like a capital A.

Considered one of the best rock exposures in the northeastern United States, Sideling Hill's syncline, formed 350 million years ago, is 850 feet high, according to the Maryland Geologic Survey. Its layers are formed from sedimentary rock. But here's the really cool thing: One-hundred million years before Pangaea, Western Maryland was covered by an inland sea. To the east, mountains stood in the area around Chesapeake Bay and Baltimore, and the sediment ran off into Western Maryland's shallow sea. Then the great continental shift came, and in Maryland, the mountains and sea more or less swapped places.

During construction, ten million tons of rock were extracted from the Sideling Hill cut, and then used to fill the east-to-west road inclines. The excavation took sixteen months, and it took another year to complete the interstate through the hill.

Exhibits at the visitor center explain the geology. If you're on I-68 west of Hancock, you can't miss it. But in case you need directions, call (301) 842-2155.

Big Fishermen
Bloomington (for lack of a closer town)

According to Wikipedia, "Grand Slam" refers to thirteen competitive sports series; six films, bands, albums, and TV series; a G.I. Joe character; a bomb; and a big, fat breakfast from Denny's.

Clearly the Wikipedians haven't heard of the Grand Slam of Trout at the North Branch of the Potomac River, south of Jennings Randolph Lake about 8 miles upstream of Bloomington in Garrett County. Here, anglers who catch four trout species—cutthroat, rainbow, brown,

(continued on page 198)

Washington's First Two Monuments

Everyone recognizes the marble-and-granite obelisk dominating Washington, D.C.'s skyline as *the* Washington Monument. Here in the Free State, where George Washington often came and went, the Father of Our Country is remembered with two more monuments. Both claim patriotic firsts: One is the nation's first Washington Monument to see construction start, and one is the first to see it finish. You see, their construction schedules overlapped.

Baltimoreans got to work on their version ten years after George's 1799 death. The cornerstone was laid in 1815 for the column crafted by Robert Mills, who went on to design the D.C. monument. Italian sculptor Enrico Causici, who had sculpted panels for the Capitol Rotunda, depicted GW's likeness for the top of the Baltimore monument. It took Causici fifteen years to complete the task. The dedication took place in late 1829. Those who climb the 228 stairs the first Thursday of every month are in for something special—admission to the balcony for a view George himself would have appreciated. This GW monument is located at 699 North Charles Street and is open Wednesday through Sunday, 10:00 a.m. to 4:00 p.m.; see www.baltimoremuseums.org/washington.html for details.

Sixty miles to the west, deep in the heart of rural Washington County, villagers gathered outside tiny Boonsboro on July 4, 1827. They laid stones for what became the first *completed* monument honoring George Washington. The barrel-shaped tower had a rough go over the next century. Seems the builders failed to use mortar. Forty years later its location near Antietam put it in harm's way during North-South hostilities. The Union Army used the monument as a signal station. In the 1930s FDR's Civilian Conservation Corps reconstructed the monument, this time using mortar. Today, hikers on the Appalachian Trail pass by. Climb the thirty-two steps for a spectacular vista of the

The nation's first completed Washington Memorial stands near Boonsboro, where patriotic villagers got to work on July 4, 1827.

Maryland countryside. Plaques describe the fall raptor migration. For more on Washington Monument State Park, call (301) 791-4767 or visit www.dnr.state.md.us/publiclands/western/washington.html.

As for the Washington Monument in our nation's capital? It began with a 1783 vote by the Continental Congress. But you know how slowly things move in Washington: The monument's capstone wasn't set until December 6, 1884.

★ ★

and brook—in a single day win the unofficial (and unrewarded) North Branch Grand Slam. Alan Klotz, fisheries biologist, says he's not aware of any other Grand Slam for other fish species in Maryland. Cutthroat and rainbow trout are westerners, and brown trout arrived from Europe. They are stocked, and join the native brook trout.

Anglers, take note! You can find more about this fab four of fishies at www.dnr.state.md.us/fisheries.

Mastodon Teeth and the Civil War

Boonsboro

Growing up near Civil War battlefields like Antietam, Doug Bast had heard the legends and seen the battlefield relics stored in local attics. But it was a childhood trip to the Smithsonian Institutions in Washington, D.C., that first drew him to weapons from any war and turned him on to the notion of opening his own museum. That he did, in 1975. Today, more than thirty years later, Bast says, "I started with the Civil War. Now I'm into every period."

It's easy to find his Boonsborough Museum of History. Look for the Victorian house at 113 North Main Street with five cannons on the front porch. Public hours are limited—from 1:00 to 5:00 p.m. on Sundays, May through September only. Call ahead for an appointment (301-432-6969), however, and Bast will do his best to accommodate you.

The rooms are jam-packed with treasures. Consider the goblets, dice, buttons, and a small Abraham Lincoln created after the Gettysburg Address. They're all carved from lead bullets by soldiers in camp. A framed flower plucked from Lincoln's coffin; a Bible used to administer the oath of allegiance to "rebels," aka Confederate soldiers (reportedly 10,000 Confederates kissed the tome); and even pikes that abolitionist John Brown hoped to arm slaves with are here.

Bast has a wood desk made of the scaffolding from which Brown, architect of the famously failed 1859 raid on the federal arsenal at nearby Harpers Ferry, West Virginia, was hanged. Maybe by the time you visit, Bast will have found a place to display it.

That's just a smidgen of what's here. Look for the cornice from the Truman-era White House renovation, fossilized mastodon tooth and woolly mammoth tusk, dinosaur bones, and Patrick Henry's framed signature. The oldest and creepiest object: a piece of a mummy wrap circa 350 BC.

If you're interested in Civil War history, you will find it in abundance. After all, Bast's the local go-to guy for memorabilia from that era. Even if your interest in the war is zilch, you still gotta see this place.

Blankets, Columns, and Soda Straws
Boonsboro

One day in 1920, workers were out doing their thing at the original quarry site for the old National Pike. (Trivia buffs note: This was along the nation's first stretch of blacktop macadam road.) Dynamiting their way through rock, they blew into what is now Crystal Grottoes Caverns. Owner Jerry Downs reports that this cave has more stalactites per square foot than any known cave in the world. Imagine unearthing such a surprise.

The public first trooped through what is Maryland's only "show cave"—a fancy way of saying "open to the public"—in 1922. Ever since, the grottoes have been on the must-see lists of generations of Marylanders (and, given the close proximity, probably Pennsylvanians, West Virginians, and Virginians, too).

Currently, you can tour 900 feet of cave, entering through an old stone house that Downs's grandfather helped to build. Cellar-type doors open to a staircase, which descend to the first "room" 8 feet belowground. Narrow paths wend through the rooms, with their mud-like walls, tender stalactites, and palpable humidity. The cavern's largest room, 20 by 30 feet, is called the Blanket Room because of the wide sheet of formation (known as a "blanket") found here. If that formation had folded, it would be called a "drapery." Other formations include "columns" (when stalagmite meets stalactite), "ribbons"

Maryland's only "show" cave is located
outside Boonsboro.

(built out of the slope of the wall), and "soda straws" (which look like their name).

The cave's original owners willed the place to Downs's grandfather in 1966, and the grottoes have been in the family ever since. You can check them out daily April through October, and weekends November through March. The caverns are about 1 mile south of U.S. Alternate 40 on Route 34. For more information, call (301) 432-6336.

Corresponding Arches
Burkittsville

At the top of a steep hill in the middle of nowhere stands a 50-foot-high structure with arched windows and a tower. It looks like a castle, or maybe an ivy-covered academic building. It's neither, but I bet you can't guess what it is.

Give up? It's a monument to war correspondents. Now part of Gathland State Park, you'll find it at the ridge of South Mountain, near Burkittsville at Crampton's Gap. George Alfred Thompson, the youngest Civil War correspondent, built the monument in 1896 on his estate. Maryland governor Lloyd Lowndes presided over the dedication in October of that year, and the names of the Civil War's 147 reporters and artists are inscribed hereupon. "Gath" was Townsend's pen name, drawn from the Bible.

If you would like more information on the monument, call (301) 371-4575 or check www.dnr.state.md.us/publiclands/western/gathland .html.

Helmets and Hawaiian Shirts
Cumberland

Cumberland, a big-league transportation hub back when the C&O Canal and National Road competed during the nineteenth century, now dwells quietly along the interstate. It's not exactly where you'd expect to pick up a Russian civilian gas mask. Or a winter hat for enlisted Russian soldiers.

Gas mask or topper? Check out Off Centre to see.

Steve Colby apparently ran into a good deal on European surplus uniforms to sell alongside Hawaiian shirts, old-school girlie calendars, and even a high-frequency medical apparatus, sans tubes, that dates to the 1920s. Kitsch is king at Off Centre, the cleverly named store at 54 North Centre Street (301-876-9002), the latest from Colby, whose merchandising march west started with a shop in Frederick and includes an Internet retail business based in Hagerstown. "I appreciate tacky," he said. As well as a good chapeau.

Shoppers in search of eccentricities: "Y'all come." Just not on Monday and Tuesday, when the shop is closed.

Rolling to Victory

It's impossible to imagine partisans for Barack Obama or John McCain constructing a giant ball to "roll" to victory. I mean, what's that about?

But in 1840, that's precisely what the Allegany County Whigs did to boost their man, William Henry "Tippecanoe" Harrison.

The 12-foot ball was built on a wood frame and covered with red, white, and blue cloth. A bar through the center extended on either side so men could push it along. Its builders, backing a movement to unseat the eighth U. S. president, Martin Van Buren, rolled the ball to a convention in Baltimore. They then loaned it to their New York brethren, who rolled it to Philadelphia, New York City, and finally to Boston. Slathered in slogans such as "Old Allegany; with heart and soul this ball we roll," the ball made the newspapers wherever it revolved, according to *Allegany County, A History,* by Stegmaier, Kershaw, and Wiseman, from which this story is taken.

The ball was so successful that it had a second act. Debuting at the three-day Grand Harrison Rally, the Great Ball drew the stares of 5,000 and required 60 men to move it, before it played to crowds in Maryland, Pennsylvania, and Virginia. The new ball's slogan: "Ye Allegany boys, come help us roll this Ball. It's grown so very large, we'll need you one and all."

It ain't the CNN/YouTube debate, is it?

In case you're wondering, Harrison beat Van Buren and took Allegany County by 178 votes. The new president passed through the county en route to Washington, D.C., where he died six weeks later.

★ ★

Goin' West
Cumberland

The National Road was built to open up the west, and you can see the very spot where the shovel hit the dirt to start construction. If you can find it, that is.

Look for the survey marker in the pedestrian island located where Greene Street makes a sharp curve instead of crossing what locals call "the blue bridge" into West Virginia. On a map, it sort of looks like the intersection of Greene Street and Greene Street.

Figuring out the National Road is almost as hard as finding the marker. State tourism official Marci Ross knows all about it, and straightened me out. First came the "bank road," as the National Pike from Baltimore to Cumberland was called. Private business paid for that. Construction of the National Road started in Cumberland in 1811 and headed west and crosses six states. It ends in Vidalia, Illinois. In Maryland, US 40 west from Cumberland is generally considered the National Road. These days, the various byways that make up the old route are known as the Historic National Road, and you can read all about Maryland's portion of it at www.visitmaryland.org.

When built, the National Road was a huge deal. Thomas Jefferson himself lobbied for it, spurred by George Washington. As a young man, Washington had used the route—previously a Native American trail—as an aide to General Braddock during the French and Indian War. "George Washington was with Braddock on that expedition, and that's where the idea of westward expansion really came from," said Ross.

Awesome.

Wheels of Fortune
Cumberland

The late James Richard Thrasher loved horse-drawn vehicles. He's been gone since 1987, but you can still feel the love in Cumberland, where the Queen City Transportation Museum at 210 Centre Street (301-777-

1776) opened to display some of his collection when the Thrasher Carriage Museum in Frostburg ran out of room.

Even though these are old-fashioned vehicles, you'll see how some things just don't change. Come here to view the late nineteenth- or early twentieth-century equivalent of, say, a '66 Mustang convertible. This would be the Oakland wagon, a spiffy-looking open carriage. The era's more practical minivan? Probably the early twentieth-century Curtain Rockaway, a black family wagon with yellow wheels and curtains.

The Queen City Transportation Museum makes a point of displaying the vehicles that traveled the nearby National Road—significant for its part in opening the frontier beyond Cumberland. The collection includes farm wagons, mining vehicles, delivery vehicles, and a sleigh on bob runners for traversing this mountainous terrain. The circa 1840 Conestoga wagon, named for the Conestoga River in Lancaster County, Pennsylvania, had a curved floor to stabilize its contents. Very interesting!

Going Its Own Way

Garrett County

Maryland's westernmost county displays the same independence as its early frontier settlers. Not only does Garrett County claim different geology from the rest of the state, but its weather marches to its own drummer, too. The contrast can be especially clear from the vantage point of next-door-neighbor Allegany County.

At an elevation of 2,000 to 3,360 feet (at Hoye Crest on Backbone Mountain, Maryland's highest point), Garrett County—well, most of it anyway—sees at least 48 inches of precipitation a year. It even gets lake-effect snow when winter winds blast from the northwest off Lake Erie clear up by Ontario, Canada. The county sits atop the Allegheny Plateau, which you begin to climb at Dans Mountain in far western Allegany County.

Translation: Allegany County sits in the plateau's rain shadow. So, even though it's mountainous, it's noticeably drier. "You can see cactus by the side of I-68 if you know what you're looking for," says

Garrett College professor Kevin Dodge. Except for its far western eleva-
tion, most of Allegany is located in the "Ridge and Valley" portion of
the state, which gets a measly 36 to 40 inches of precipitation, according to the state Department of Natural Resources.

About 60 percent of Garrett County has another distinction. Unlike
the rest of the state, its streams don't flow to Chesapeake Bay. Atop
a rise on I-68 at Green Lantern Road in far eastern Allegany County,
a sign announces the end of the Eastern Continental Divide. That's
the boundary between rainfall draining east into Chesapeake Bay, and
rainfall draining west into the Mississippi River and Gulf of Mexico. So,
if you shower in Garrett County, look for the runoff in New Orleans,
Louisiana.

Old Stones
Grantsville

Betcha been wondering where the world's largest single-span stone
bridge was built in 1813. You got it—Maryland. When the 80-foot
Casselman River Bridge was constructed along the National Road, it
was such a marvel that folks just waited for it to come tumbling down.
Sorry, folks: It's now the centerpiece of a lovely four-acre state park and
abuts the Spruce Forest Artisan Village, a collection of (mostly) old log
houses-cum-studios moved to the site. You can find it on US Alt. 40.

Casselman River Bridge State Park can be contacted through the
New Germany State Park office at 349 Headquarters Lane in Grants-
ville, or by calling (301) 895-5453. The Web site is www.dnr.state.md
.us/publiclands/western/casselman.html.

Of Artists and Log Cabins
Grantsville

Gary Yoder works in a log cabin that's older than the entire country.
Indeed he does, one in the collection of old mountain buildings that
have been moved over the years to Spruce Forest Artisan Village. Visit
May through October, if possible, because that's when artists and

An early American feat of engineering, the Casselman Bridge was built in 1813.

craftspeople open their studios so you can watch them work. You can also examine the architecture if you like. Yoder certainly has. "I sit here in the cabin and think about how they built it," the well-known bird artist said of the circa 1775 Markley House, where he works. It was moved here from nearby Pennsylvania, where it was built by the Markleys, a couple who had an 800-acre land grant from the king of England. Yoder surmises that horses, oxen, and block and tackle helped to build the two-story cabin. "Massive white pine logs; they were green and heavy and these people probably didn't have a lot of neighbors," he said.

Old log cabins find new homes at Spruce Forest
Artisan Village.

The Spruce Village potter's studio used to be a National Road inn
frequented by drovers, the old-timey word for livestock drivers. Alta's
Cabin, named for founder Alta Schrock, was her childhood writing
cabin. Also here are an 1835 home that serves as an Anabaptist Peace
Center, and the restored and operating Stanton's Mill that dates to
1797.

Spruce Forest is part of the Penn Alps complex that includes a
next-door restaurant, and it's all located alongside the Casselman
River Bridge. The village, at 177 Casselman Road (301-895-3332;
www.spruceforest.org), preserves Appalachiana both culturally and
architecturally.

A Giant's Big Red Rocker

Hagerstown

Remember giant coffeepots atop breakfast joints or mighty men mad about mufflers outside car repair shops? The owners of the Hagerstown Furniture Outlet apparently do. Some years back, its roof sprouted a giant red rocking chair. Sixteen feet high and made of pressure-treated yellow pine, the chair's parts were hoisted onto the outlet's roof for assembly. Now, when anyone hears the ad, "under the giant red rocking chair," they won't have to strain their eyes on the heavy commercial road.

The address is 13402 Pennsylvania Avenue, on the off chance the rocking chair doesn't work for you.

Midnight Snacks

Hagerstown

Why are all those people lined up in a back alley between 7:00 p.m. and 2:00 a.m.? They must be up to no good.

But not if the alley is behind the house at 912 Maryland Avenue. Locals know that's the only time to eat hot out-of-the-fryer confections from Krumpe's Do-Nut Shop (301-733-6103 or www.krumpesdonuts .com). Located in the house's former garage, it's affixed to the Krumpe bakery. And night time is the right time for making those yummy sugar-coated, powdered, filled with one-of-four flavors, or glazed goodies. At 2:00 a.m., the shop shuts down and the delivery trucks head out.

Night after night, the third and fourth generations of doughnut-making Krumpes crank out the family's finest, 120 dozen per hour, 600 to 700 dozen per night.

Owners Rudy and Fred Krumpe grew up in the business, which traces its lineage to their grandfather. Their father branched off and took over the distribution part of the business. The alley doughnut shop arrived later, behind what was then the family home. "We took out trash for the doughnut shop," said Fred. "That's how we made

★ ★

The flour flies late at Krumpe's, Hagerstown's iconic doughnut shop. JANE MARIE KRUMPE

our allowance." The shop began after folks started sniffing around—literally—during nighttime production hours. And it's become a Hagerstown institution.

"When people move away, they say, 'This is the first place I came when I got home from college,'" said Rudy. A group of Princeton University frat pledges once found their way to the alley, tasked with bringing back the fabled fare. The biggest time of year for Krumpes comes the night before Fastnaught Day, the traditional German start to Lent, aka Shrove Tuesday or Mardi Gras. Folks have been known to offer $10 for a place in line. The demand is so high, the Krumpes work almost round the clock. "It's the craziest two days of the year," said Fred.

Mobile Tomes

Little-known fact: The nation's first bookmobile fired up in Hagerstown.

Well, that might be an overly twenty-first-century description of what happened. In actuality, a Library Wagon was conceived, commissioned, and constructed. It had, as librarian Mary Titcomb wrote, "shelves on the outside and a place for storage of cases in the center resembled somewhat a cross between a grocer's delivery wagon and the tin peddlers cart of by gone New England days." That's a rather specific description, wouldn't you say? Mr. Thomas, the janitor, drove the wagon and dispensed the books.

In April 1905, the wagon rolled. Miss Titcomb's descriptions of the Washington County Free Library's wagon are priceless. They had to paint it an upbeat red after one rural reader warned off the "dead wagon," as no deaths had recently occurred at his place. It delivered throughout the rural county for five years before a freight train smashed it to bits. Only then came the "motorized book wagon," which, naturally, is a bit more twenty-first century.

In *The Story of the Washington County Free Library,* parts of which I read at www.whilbr.org/bookmobile/index.aspx, Miss Titcomb basks in her county's achievement. And it's definitely a good one. I can't remember the last time I saw a bookmobile, but remind me to go looking as soon as I finish writing this book.

Boggling the Mind
Near McHenry (in Garrett County)

What happens when a piece of the Ice Age gets stuck in the present? Come to Cranesville Swamp west of McHenry to find out. It was formed nearly 15,000 years ago and is home to plants that usually dwell in northernmost Alaska and Canada. Here stand the world's southernmost tamarack trees, along with a lot of other cool stuff.

Scientists can date the bog's age because peat preserves pollen. The oldest pollen samples come from species typically associated with cold northern tundra. Which proves the point: Cranesville Swamp is a little bit of the Ice Age trapped in modern-day Maryland.

The odd bog resulted when Ice Age species struggled to stay in suitable habitat during the big melt. (The ice never made it as far south as Maryland, but the thermometer still nosedived.) The elements conspired to help them do so in the Cranesville area, which is a depression lying 400 feet below the surrounding 2,900-foot hills. Colder air settles in the swamp at night to create a frost pocket. So, frosts arrive earlier and leave later than in surrounding areas—ergo, cold-climate plants like cranberry, and the insect-eating round-leaved sundew. "The plants that continue to do well in Cranesville are probably those that got outcompeted elsewhere," said Kevin Dodge, professor at Garrett College. "These plants are adapted to a shorter growing season."

Northern bird species like migratory alder flycatchers thrive here, and the tiny saw-whet owl nests at Cranesville. The massive peat bog straddles the West Virginia–Maryland border. For directions, go to www .nature.org/wherewework/northamerica/states/maryland/preserves/ art135.html.

A "mountain coaster" sends visitors on an adventure at Wisp. LORI EPP, WISP RESORT

Coasting Along

McHenry

Roller coasters are supposed to have names like Cyclone and Space Mountain, and you find them in Coney Island and Disney World—right?

Heck, rules are made to be broken. Take the Mountain Coaster at Wisp Resort, a spot known mostly for skiing. The coaster, a German export, is the only one of its kind in the Mid-Atlantic and the fourth in the United States. It's not an old-fashioned roller coaster. But since it climbs 1,300 feet uphill and shoots its riders back down over 3,500 feet, "coaster" seems as good a name as any.

The folks at Wisp consider it a "gravitational hybrid" of an Alpine slide and a roller coaster. That's good news for riders who can't stomach a true-blue roller coaster. The two-person carts allow the riders to control speed. According to Wisp, a centrifugal braking system limits speed to 26 miles per hour downhill.

My luck, I visited in a downpour and the coaster was down for maintenance. So I didn't get a ride. But I was a) glad to hear about that individual speed control, b) intrigued that a pulley carries the car uphill and the rider controls the release as gravity starts pulling the cart down, and c) pretty darned impressed to hear that skiers have been hitching rides on the coaster for a rest break from the slopes or to maximize their time on Wisp's mountain.

The resort, located in McHenry at 296 Marsh Hill Road, offers additional info at www.wispresort.com or (301) 387-4911.

All Terrain

McHenry

Where do you go if the river's too low? If you're a white-water enthusiast, why up the mountain to an amazing place where nature doesn't get in the way of a good run.

Adventure Sports Center International (ASCI) opened in 2007 to wide-eyed amazement. Here we have the world's only mountaintop white-water course. Not only that, but the 1,700-foot-long recirculating course has a drop of up to 24 vertical feet. It also has the capacity to crank the water up to Class IV rapids. Wow! Since it's man-made, that means adjustments for novices can be made down to Class II/III. (ASCI clinics are advised for beginners.) How does it work? Pumps push water up through the winding concrete and natural boulder course. It took two years to build and required the excavation of forty million pounds of rock. Interesting factoid: Some "rocks" weighed up to eighty tons.

ASCI is all about creating a major-league adventure sports mecca, and offers several rafting and kayaking options. The center includes

550 acres where rock climbers can take on natural sandstone outcroppings. ASCI is just up the mountain from the base operations at Wisp at 250 Adventure Sports Way (877-300-2724; www.adventuresports center.com).

Bear with Us
Oakland

If a tree falls in the forest and nobody's there to hear, we've gotta wonder if it made a noise. If a tree falls in one of the burgeoning number of yards in the growing Deep Creek Lake resort area, you can bet the buzz of a chain saw is close behind. And it's often used to transform trees into bears.

Here in Bear Country, chain-saw sculptors routinely carve logs and old stumps into bears. You see them everywhere: In front of homes. In front of businesses. They're standing along the walking trail in Oakland, chain-saw carver Shelly Uphole's hometown. Yep, she carved those, including a whimsical three-bear piece. A baby bear sleeps inside the tree, one hides, and a curious third checks out a honey-filled beehive. "The log offered itself as doing those three. The honeycomb adds a little bit of story," Shelly told me.

She gives a lot of thought to her creations. "Sometimes the log will offer itself as a particular animal or person. You can look at that log and see it before you ever start carving," she said. Before she sets blade to wood, she blocks out the figure's elements, like the head. "Start at the top and work your way down. Almost carve it in your mind first."

And then, she fires up the chain saw. You might catch Shelly at work around the community (please note that she works within a safety perimeter) or you can look for her at Autumn Glory, the big mid-October festival in Oakland, which you can find out about at www.visitdeepcreek.com.

"I'm just a small-town girl God's blessed with a gift," said Shelly. "And I like to share, especially with kids."

Bears chainsawed from logs emerge from old trees around Garrett County.

★ ★

Burgers and Buckwheat Cakes

Oakland

There's white stuff on the framed faces lining the walls at Dottie's Grill and Soda Fountain. What is it? Shaving cream? Bubble bath?

No, it's whipped cream, evidence of a treasured birthday tradition here at this truly local breakfast and lunch hot spot in the back of Englander's, a sizable antiques emporium. If you've been "creamed" at Dottie's, you've been embraced as a local. That's a big deal in Garrett County, where heads turn in winter when non-locals arrive at Dottie's counter. Come summer, as Dottie Uphold puts it, "People like my regulars stay clear because you can never find a place to sit down."

Englander's Antique Mall used to be Englander's, the local drugstore. Now, customers browse through shelves brimming with everything you can imagine. Spotted recently: a 1926 diploma from Akron High School's vocational educational program as well as a Roseville pottery section. Devotees of Dottie's cooking include anyone who appreciates a hamburger for under $3 or fans of the region's unique "buckwheat cakes," which are pancakes made with sourdough. And everyone knows when summer's arrived because milk shakes—made with real ice cream—disappear out the front door.

As for getting creamed? It could happen to anyone: Local kids. A nearby town's mayor. Even the county state's attorney. Once, an out-of-town bank executive was in on his birthday. Someone asked Dottie, "You gonna cream him?" She replied, "Oh, I couldn't do that." After all, the man wore a nice suit (and was from out of town). But tradition dies hard out here in the mountains, and the executive was creamed—lightly. "Every time he comes back, he checks to make sure his picture is on the wall," said Dottie.

If you want to get creamed, head to Dottie's—and Englander's—at 204 East Alder Street (301-533-0000).

* *

Falling Water

Oakland

Maryland's highest free-falling waterfall is located in one of the state's last virgin hemlock forests. Between 54 and 63 feet of water cascade over 300-million-year-old rocks at Muddy Creek Falls, which include cross-bedded sandstones and more easily eroded siltstones and shales—or at least that's what the Maryland Geological Survey says. On an early spring day when Muddy Creek is running fast and high on its way into the Youghiogheny River, there's nothing prettier than its offspring falls.

The falls are located in Swallow Falls State Park at 222 Herrington Lane, and are a fine starting point for a walk that continues past rocks to the smaller, but just as pretty, Swallow Falls. For info in summer call (301) 387-6938; the winter number is (301) 334-9180. And while you're there, imagine Thomas Edison, Henry Ford, Harvey Firestone, and John Burroughs roughing it at this spot. That was back when these captains of industry camped around the country in style and called themselves the "Vagabonds."

Draft Logging

Oldtown

Henry Maier of Oldtown met his buddy Leo Eby over a bad batch of mulch—it happens. Bad mulch, that is. Well, friendship, too. What bloomed from Henry's wilted flowers is a match made in draft horse heaven.

You see, when Leo went over to Henry's to see about the garden, he spotted a pair of Belgian draft horses named Baron and Prince out in the field. Leo himself had a couple of draft horses—a breed called Percherons—named Barney and Bob. The two men got to talking, and before long they'd teamed up to harvest timber at a friend's place. Now, harvesting timber with draft horses has become a hobby with the duo.

Maryland's highest falls tumble in Swallow Falls State Park.

Taking out trees, or "skidding," is done more selectively via draft animals than by machine. "That's the plus for the harvest," said Henry. "The fact you can walk your horses between trees."

"It keeps your timber assets in a sustainable way," Leo added. In other words, a property owner can select trees that are ready to harvest, take them out, earn the income from them, and protect the surrounding trees in their woods. If the wood is used for a practical purpose—say, for flooring, as Henry did at his house—you end up with a negative carbon footprint. And these days, as we all know, that's a good thing.

The pair (along with Baron, Prince, Barney, and Bob) occasionally demonstrates their logging skills at area events such as the Western Maryland Forestry Logger's Field and Equipment Day. Henry also uses his horses for hayrides and sleigh rides at local functions. Keep an eye on the local newspaper to see if you can catch them.

I won't be surprised if Leo figures out how to log with oxen. He's been training two, named Lion and Tiger (total weight: nearly 5,000 pounds), in a wooden yoke, just like the early Western Maryland settlers used.

index

index

index

index

index

index

index

index

index

index

index

about the author

Allison Blake is a longtime regional writer who has lived in Maryland for almost half of her life. She is the author of *The Chesapeake Bay Book* and lives in Mitchellville—except when it's cold, when she hides out in New Orleans.

CPSIA information can be obtained
at www.ICGtesting.com
Printed in the USA
LVOW13s1713150617
538255LV00010B/807/P